# Visual Signals
## Issue Two

SEPT-OCT 2020 ISSUE

# Updates

Visual Signals is now on Patreon! I've been talking to some of the folks over at the other Vaporwave themed Zine, Private Suite, and it just seems to make sense to turn Visual Signals into a Patreon project. Mainly because this allows you to get each issue in the mail without the hassle of remembering and also keeps this project alive. Interestingly enough, it seems the first issue (ISSUE ZERO) was a huge hit, but ISSUE ONE barely got 1/10th of the support.

I love the collaboration of working with other writers, interviewing artists and labels and sharing the latest in the scene. I really don't want anyone to miss out on all the hard work every issue requires. So the Patron makes the most sense. So now you'll notice a list

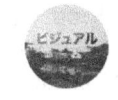

**Visual Signals**
is creating A Monthly Vapor and
Aesthetic Cultural Zine

of name in the front and back of each issue, depending on the tier you too could have your name printed with every issue for as low as 3 USD. More information at:
https://www.patreon.com/visualsignals

In other news, I sent out a survey asking what people thought about the zine. Overall, it was positive feedback but one thing that was dragging behind was overall design. This zine originally was supposed to be a simple digest but now I want it to be more. So in this issue you'll see a couple of new design changes. First article titles are fully themed to the article. Second, we now have the ability to print full page width. It's a little extra work but we think it's going to make the articles and content pop.

In the future I might invest in adobe illustrator but I'm already paying for AE and PS, so if you'd like to see this project evolve into better aesthetics, supporting Visual Signals is the best way to help. We have T-shirts, the Patreon now and just simple word of mouth. If you bought a copy, tweeting a photo of the zine is extremely helpful. Did you know Pad Chennington posted a photo of issue one on Reddit and it got over 1k upvotes. Like that's insane.

As for personal life, I'm still doing the 41 day meditation program. I just decided that the 5am wake up call will be part of my life. I also recently ordered a Penny skateboard as I want to see more of SF but it's larger than it looks and I think by wheels I'll get to see more. Which is actually a good thing for the zine because so far all of the covers have been from my abroad photography. It would be cool to put some cover art from my new city.

Speaking of the new city, Nekkun came up from San Jose this month. We made a little video about his new label, Kanga Corp, which can be found on YouTube or in podcast form on Spotify. We hand delivered me their first cassette and we just hung out for the day. The last time I hung out with anyone from the Vapor-scene was when I went to Japan (which oddly enough, there's a couple articles about that trip in this issue). That was over a year ago.

Outside of IRL, http://visualsignals.xyz, now has all digital copies available online to read for free. No downloads *but if you want a PDF for 3USD on the Patreon it's yours*. Check out the website cause I spent a good amount of time working on it.

Anyways, thanks for grabbing a copy of issue two. If you are missing a copy of issue zero or one, they are and will always be on Amazon. That's the beauty of printing on demand. Thanks everyone for the support and thanks for the following Patreon Supporters.

## Patreon "温" VIP

Nekkun
Sheep

— —

Jason VanSlycke
eye click
Rich Siegel
Chiefahleaf
Com_Zepol

https://www.patreon.com/visualsignals

Follow This Project on Twitter:
@SignalsVisual

围棋 KAIFU

9月から10月
日本の月間天気

DIGITAL ARTIST SPOTLIGHT
|| TAKUCHI

THE MACHINE IN THE GHOST:
THE DIGITAL WORLD IS THE SPIRITUAL WORLD
ゴースト・イン・ザ・シェル

BIG
MUSIC PROMOTERS WITH THEIR SMALL WAYS TO
PROMOTE
PETRIDISCH
FAN COLLECTION

5 HORROR-THEMED ALBUMS FOR
HALLOWEEN

PITCH SHIFTER
ONE YEAR LATER

学习中文
LEARN CHINESE

NICKELODEON
降击神通
AVATAR
THE LAST AIRBENDER

X LO-FI
HIP-HOP

VISUAL
ビジュアル SIGNALS
merch

SCENE NEWS
ニュース

OUTSTANDING #3
DESIGN AWARD

PAST CONCERTS
& NEW
NOTEWORTHY

AKIHABARA
SEGA CLOSED ARCADE

佐藤博 HIROSHI SATOH
THIS BOY

bandcamp
TOP RELEASES

BEHIND THE NAME

THE BRIDGE TO
VAPORWAVE
IN THE VIRTUAL SPACE

THOM HOSKIN
OF DONOR LENS INTERVIEW

# BIG MUSIC PROMOTERS WITH THEIR SMALL WAYS TO PROMOTE

By Zico

To release music goes three ways in this perspective; on the artists' self, with a label (or collective), and asking a promoter to get your music out there. Surely there's live streaming, and more promotions in their social media pages, though in this case will be put aside.

In the vaporwave and future funk scene, there is obviously no exception; they all reign supreme from Funky Panda and TriangleMusic to Artzie Music and Real Love Music. To be a go-to site to enjoy the music from a listener's perspective, and an artists' go-to site to share their music, the way different promoters are viewed is what revolves around them; from what music they promote, to how they promote it.

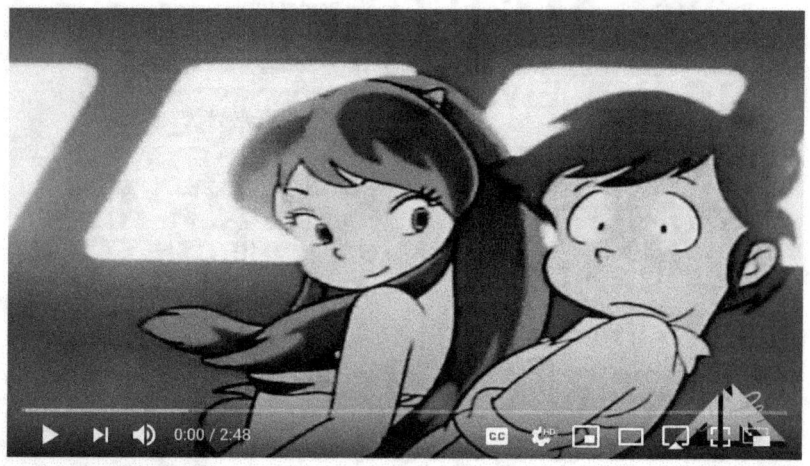

▶ ▶| ◀)) 0:00 / 2:48                    CC ⮌ ⊡ ▢ ⟆ ⟦⟧ ⛰

TANUKI - BABYBABYの夢

12,433,938 views · Jan 23, 2015          👍 151K  👎 2.6K  ↗ SHARE  ≡₊ SAVE  •••

For instance, Artzie Music, TriangleMusic, and Real Love Music utilize GIFs (moving images), sometimes with pulsating waveform bars, and then the music. They all have been well-known for using GIFs from anime old and new, sometimes retro commercials as well, not only to fit the vaporwave/future funk aesthetics of Japanese culture, but to attract diverse fans of anime, nostalgia, vaporwave, and then some. In some cases, some of their videos gained so much in popularity that the origin of the GIF itself has gone through a resurgence of viewers and fans, especially with retro anime. And then, the music coinciding with the looping GIF of a retro anime girl dancing.

As with any other new promoter, channel, company, label, and so forth, one ought to start small and then think tall. We came from Vektroid, Saint Pepsi, Cat System Corp, and AQUA FINA, all the way to Vantage, FIBRE, Tupperwave, and George Clanton. Even some of the artists in the scene like Vantage, George Clanton, and Yung Bae have gained mainstream attention, going by leaps and bounds, some signing big record deals from Warner to Arista and Sony.
Either way, artists big or small, young or old, rookies or veterans, ought to strive to get their music out there, and often would seek a label or even a well-known music promoter.

But how can a promoter do it without the use of a GIF? What is another way without the pulsating waveform bars some perceive as overused? Perhaps the artist could come up with a music video, though ought to be considered time-consuming and takes a lot of effort to put in and feed through. Even so, some artists would happily do so, than have another Sailor Moon GIF.

And then there's the problem with "variety" of music; whether it's the same artist and/or genre. Some would prefer the promoter as a destination for a specific one, while others would be turned off with it being the same thing over and over.

At this rate, it is up to the listener to judge upon variety and how promoters promote their music. Without the need for music videos, it would be the only way to promote, and to keep promoting is to promote music that connects to what it signifies for.

# DIGITAL ARTIST SPOTLIGHT

## ⫼TAKUCHI

**1. How did you get into the vaporwave scene?**

I've seen it on SNS for several years, and I knew something about the visual aspects.

I knew it properly when some Neon city records arrived at HMV in Shibuya on April 30, 2019. I bought a MoeShop vinyl and went home to study a lot. I remember it well because it is the last day of the Japanese era "平成 Heisei".

**2. You release a lot of your mixes on cassette with KillerKillerRecords. In japan, how do you make your own cassettes?**
KILLERKILLER Records are all handmade. In Japan, cassette culture is still small, so there is no cheaper manufacturer. All mixes are recorded from Vinyl.

**3. A lot of people know you for your art style, what is your characters' names?**

They have no name. Almost everything is different. The girl with cat ears are collectively called "Nekoko". I also make Nekoko dolls.

**4. What's the inspiration behind the "naughty" positions for your characters?**

It comes out naturally while drawing "Kawaii" with innocence and danger. The sophistication required for so-called "Eros" is intentionally excluded.

**5.What tools you use to create your digital art?**

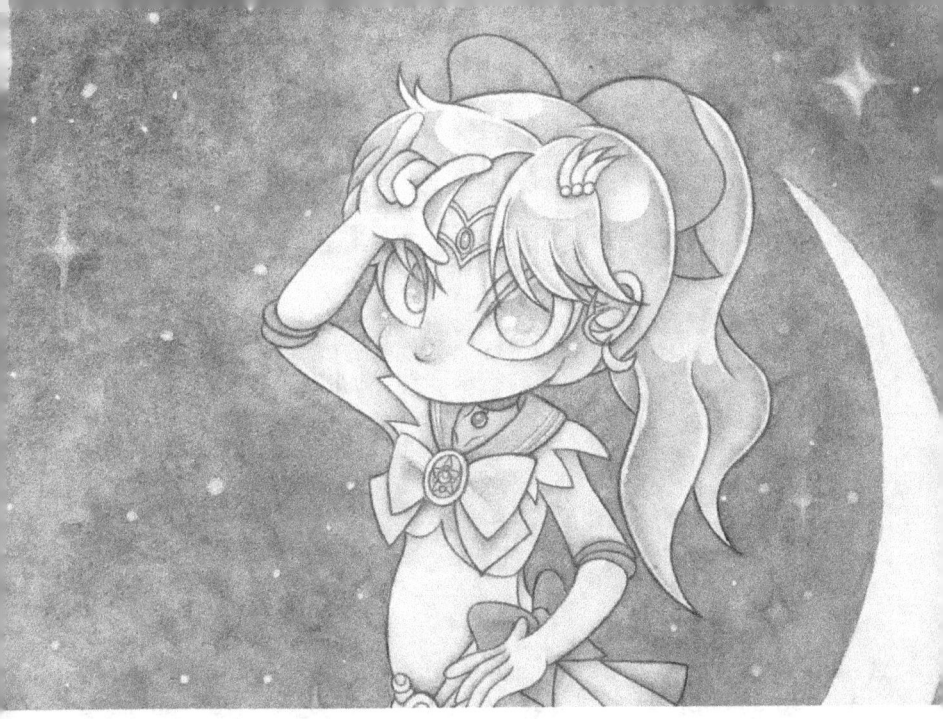

I rarely draw digital art except for jackets. For digital, I use Clip Studio. Mainly used painting materials are Japanese painting materials "水干絵具 dyed mud pigment" and colored pencils. It's not traditional usage.

**6. In Japan, how famous is your art? Has it been in any art shows or in magazines?**

It's a niche work, so it's not so famous. I mainly present my works at solo and group exhibitions. There are many exhibits at the gallery "Art complex center of tokyo" to which I belong. The next solo exhibition is scheduled for January 2021.

**7. What is your artistic dream?**

To continue painting. It's more important to me to keep drawing for myself than to become famous.

You can find more of takuchi's art and music on twitter @takuchi69.

# PETRIDISCH
## FAN COLLECTION

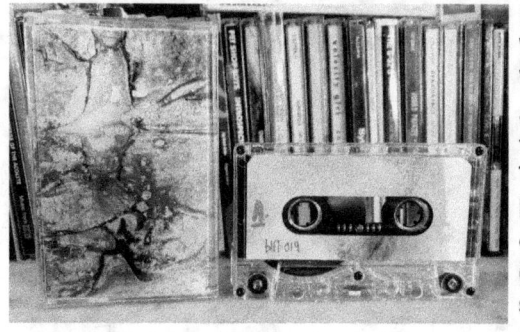

### Live in Tucson 2009 by Windy & Carl

Windy & Carl have been a very long standing favorite duo of mine. They make this sort of hazy, droney, reverbed-out guitar-and-bass (and sometimes voice) space music that is simply of another world. When they released this fragile-yet-massive full-length 2009 live set recording on tape, I had to get it. It is such an amazing document. All the art is hand-painted by Windy of the group. Not like stamps, there's some real *paint* on these things. Holding the j-card is like holding an art canvas! No two of the 150-copy pressing are alike! (HOW long did that TAKE? ;)) I love the detail and pastel-and-metallic swirl that the paint creates, very much like W&C's shifting, shimmering tunes on the tape. The set is a stunning 'career overview', punctuated by the sound of trains going by now and again.

### Souvenir Cassette by After Dinner

One of those very special things that you feel you missed out on over the years and a chance comes up again! I feel like I've always wanted this 1988 live one-off After Dinner cassette, and in fact saw it a bunch of times when I first started collecting tapes - and always passed, and later regretted. A copy was secured once my label, Fish Prints, went ahead and reissued it! This thing is built like a tank, old-school clear-and-black case but highly well made, and beautiful (and intriguing!) liner and issue notes, with stellar golden tape labels. The music here goes without saying is a mythical beast. Unbeatable live recordings chopped up with found-on-tour sounds made to sound like a full live set, issued as a "Souvenir" for those in the know at the time. Even the label logos (ReR Megacorp) look mythical and beastly when applied here.

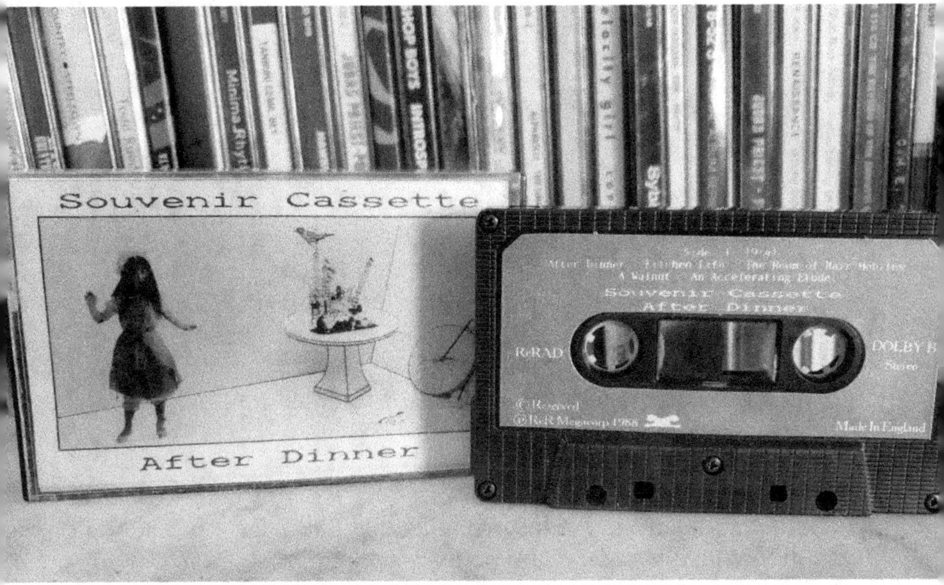

**electroniconversations by various artists**

More lore-worthy (to me) than even the 100% Electronicon tapes issued at the festivals was this hand-passed (at the first event) compilation tape on Halcyon called Electroniconversation. It basically represents what I see as an essential document of what was happening in the vaporwave scene at the time, a real fresh vitality on every track, everyone obviously giving it their all. It also certainly was the introduction for me to a HUGE chunk of happening artists - not only that the presentation is out of this world. Each of these tapes was hand-made and assembled, beautifully printed on glossy (!!!) stock paper with a purple tape.

The high-contrast yet warm nature of the artwork is some of the most sympathetic I've seen for a compilation. Bravo cityman900 and Halcyon Tapes!

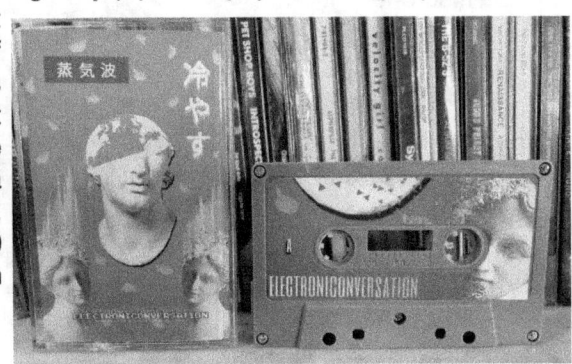

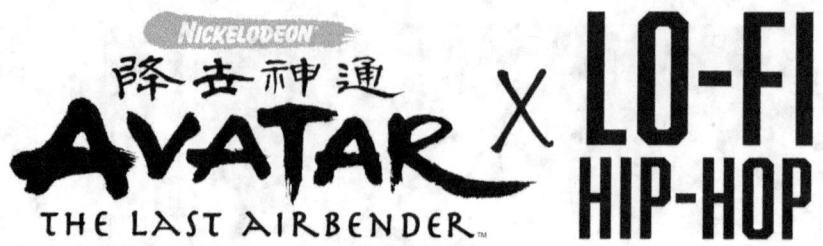

If you were a kid during the early 2000s, you'll be very familiar with the everlasting impact the nickelodeon TV show Avatar had on you. From the wisdom of Ihor to the life lessons of coming to terms with your own destiny, to say the Last Airbender was bigger than just a cartoon is an understatement.

In the year the show started I was 13 years old. It ran from 2005 to the last episode (of the main series) airing in 2008. During that age, I was more into sneaking a late hour showing of adult swim but any time Avatar came on the TV I felt at peace and found no problem watching a series that probably was aimed at a younger generation. At that time Nickelodeon wasn't known for its anime (has it ever?), so in a way the TV show kind of felt softer than most. Yet some how, years later of all the Toonami I binged in my teens, it's the Avatar soundtrack I keep returning to.

To my surprise there is an entire section of Youtube dedicated to remixing the Last Airbender into lo-fi classics. Recently I've been using them to focus at work during the stressful 4th quarter we are entering into. It's nice to heard Ihor tell me everything is going to be alright from various soundbites. The Avatar OST works too well with Lo-fi so check it out.

Here's a few I recommend:

- 1 HR Uncle Iroh Inspiration 🔥 Avatar Lofi Study Beats
- The Last Airbender | Avatar Lofi Mix
- C H I L L B E N D I N G — *Vol.* 1 — **Avatar Lofi Chill-Hop Mixtape**
- Dear Katara (Avatar's Love but it's lofi hip hop)

# NightScript's DSi & 3DS HACKS GUIDE

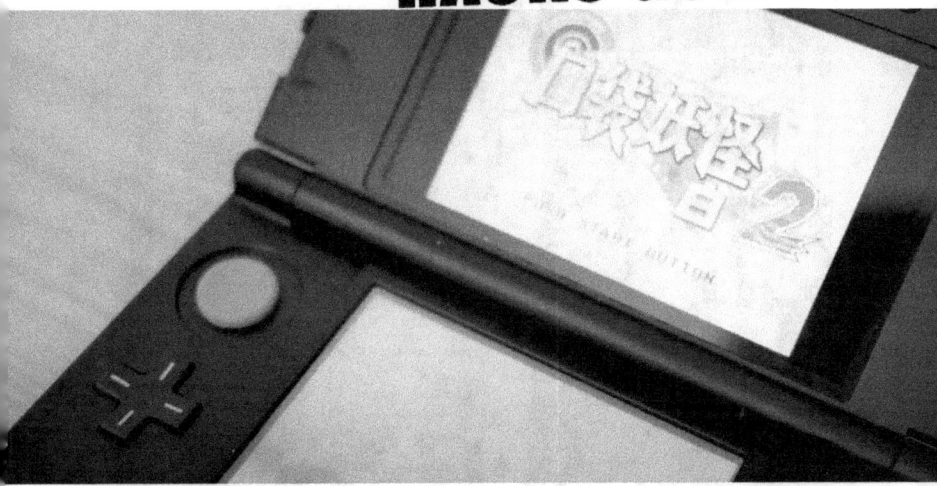

Have you ever wanted to watch movies on the go? How about playing modifications of your favorite Nintendo game? You can do that and so much more on your Nintendo consoles, thanks to the world of Homebrew. The process of modding a Nintendo DSi or a Nintendo 3DS is very easy too. All you have to do is follow the community guides, but once you're done, you have opened a world of possibilities.

Importing out-of-region? Region-Locking is removed so feel free to play Speeding up karts in Mario Kart? Cheats allow you to change anything in RAM, which means you can play at 300cc (take that Mario Kart 8). Taking screenshots of your favorite in-game moments? Luma3DS includes a screen capture feature.

Get started today by following the community-maintained guides:

- Nintendo DSi Hacking Guide: https://dsi.cfw.guide/
- Nintendo 3DS Hacking Guide: https://3ds.hacks.guide/

These guides will take you from any stock device into a fully modded console, using the best tools available (TWiLight Menu++ for the Nintendo DSi and Luma3DS for the Nintendo 3DS)

# Now Available On Amazon!

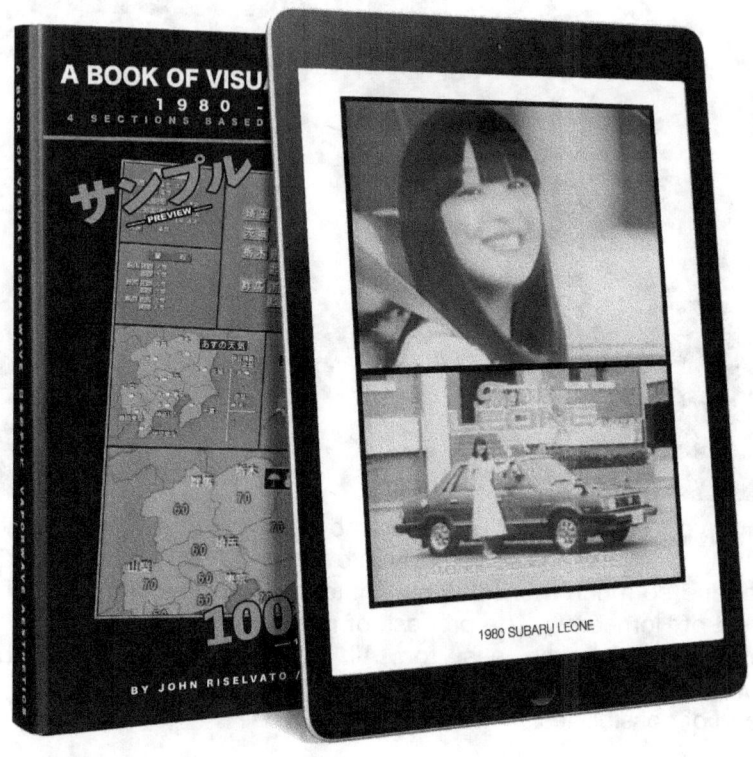

"A Book of Visual Signalwave" is the experience, feels and emotions found in Japanese television from the years 1980 to 2001. The world of Signalwave and its music has always had a visual side. This book is a contribution to the music genre in a different way with a focus on a period of time, the commercials, tv and cars. This book is pure Signalwave for the eyes! Over over 90 pages of commercials turned into comic book form. Each commercial should be viewed as an individual art piece that evokes emotional ties felt in Vaporwave.

**Available in Paperback and Kindle**

# SCENE<sup>NEWS</sup>ニュース

**Luxury Elite announces new album, *High Society***

In the beginning of the month, we were surprised with a revealing tweet from vapor legend, Luxury Elite. They announcing their newest album title as High Society and dropping that they've held onto this album for album two years. Stating they've held on to this album "for when [they were]

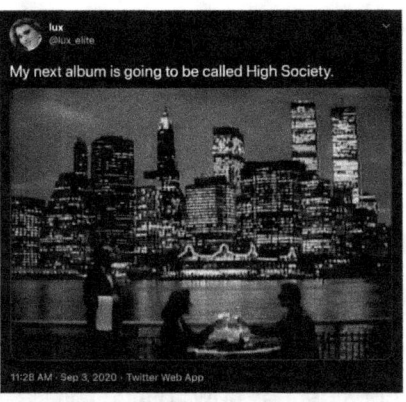

finally ready to return." Can't wait to see how the album pushes the genre!

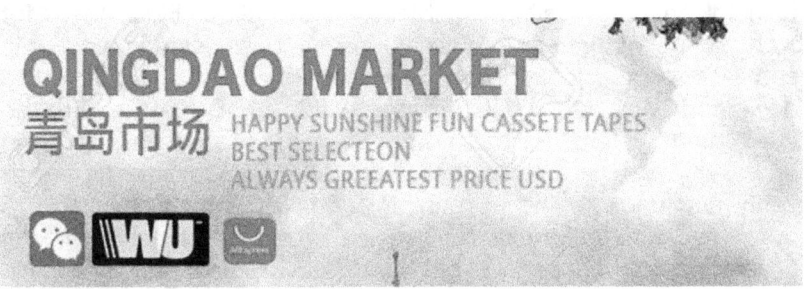

## QINGDAO MARKET

There's a new label in the scene that is the next best thing since the invention of Porter Vong (and I'm not saying that because of asian things, it's the personalities behind the projects). QINGDAO MARKET is our local knockoff vaporwave label for all things bootleg. Not only are they releasing fake version of albums, they are running the song through filters to deteriorated and ultimately completely change the tracks. Really it's impressive and a project I wish I could have thought of. - "no need to pay scalp price for rare vapor waves tapes!!"

apparently, in November we'll be seeing a boot of esprit's virtua.zip, which even has an image of George Clanton on it but this time themed to failed PSX mascot, Bubsy. There's a lot of hype behind this label and I can't wait to see what they think of next.

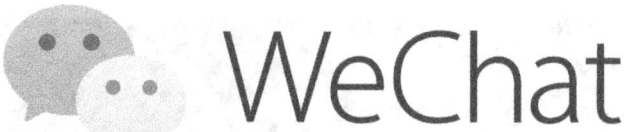

**WeChat's getting banned in the USA!**
Probably doesn't affect most but I've been using WeChat to stay in communications with my friends back in Shenzhen every day since 2017. The good news is Trump is just banning it from being on the app stores and from what I can tell, I haven't lost any functionality. I do worry that when I return to China something might happen to my account between then and now. Which is really scary considering how difficult it is to obtain and keep a WeChat account. My account is tied to my Chinese bank account, my hospital information, etc. For a foreigner, those things are painstakingly impossible to obtain without either living there for work or being there on business. Even businessmen accounts some times get blocked for no reason. So even if you wanted to download WeChat, chances are within that first week, the automated system will ban you until you upload a passport and prove who you are. Even then, you'll need a Chinese citizen to verify and unblock the account for you. It's not an easy app to obtain, so for those who do have it… it's kind of nerve racking seeing these bans coming from the US government. To say a life in china without WeChat is no life at all is an understatement. This will hit hard for those who rely on it if things get worse.

**The Story of Vaporwave - Nobody Here Doc News**
It's been a little quiet since Corona hit but I wanted to let everyone know the documentary is still in the works. The guys over at MPF are still setting up visual interview calls. We had some this week. Things are slower but not dead. Someone is here.. working on it.

### Got news?
Did we miss any news or have something to announce for next month? Send us an email at contact@musicsthehangup.com

# PAST CONCERTS

**Vaporspace StL & Culture Agency present: VAPORSPACE CULTURE WORLDWIDE**

A 2 night special of some of the most experimental sounds coming out of Culture Agency. The half hour I spent there, we were

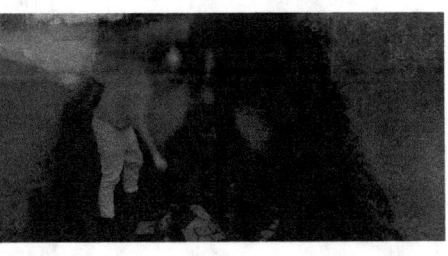

presented with some of the trippiest visuals, like "The Mall". My introduction to his sound was with eyes freaking out and a smashing of a cellphone. The music is semi screaming behind these upbeat chiptune-like tracks. I'm super loving the style and visuals. I like the mellow screaming like this but the electronic fits perfect. Here's a couple of visuals that grabbed me during his set:

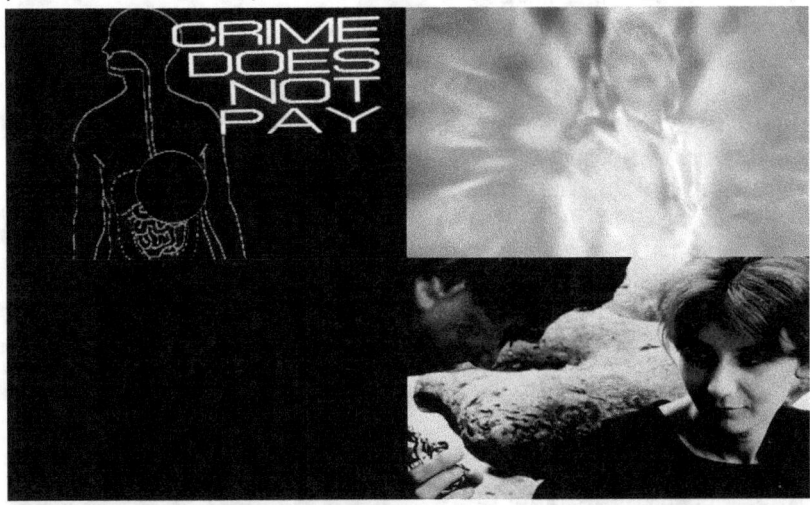

Manapool came on shortly after with some super smooth breakcore. I've actually never heard of any music like this before, but it's upbeat enough to keep you focused while calm enough to be good background music. I think it's perfect work / study music if you're looking for some from the vapor scene.

## Flamingo Fest - 9/12/2020

I literally had this on the entire day. I started just before Strawberry Station and kept into the night. The amount of talent that came out that night was incredible. Indy did an amazing job organizing this. I think my favorite visuals were the Baywatch and that small cut where Hasselhoff listens to Sarahs cassette. That was an awesome transition. Awesome day overall. Oh, did I mention my Death Note Visual Signals CM played right before Tupperwaves set! It's on YouTube if you want to watch it. Congrats IndyAdvant for organizing on such a impactful show.

## ZUYOR Vol. 7 - 9/27/2020

I originally met Japanese DJ (Future Funk), ZUYO, in Japan at the Pitch Shifter concert. Actually, the Japanese crew (ZUYOR, Ta-ke, 2x School girl, & others) and our crew all went out to dinner one night. Regardless, the 25th of Sept *ZUYOR,* the first concert she's holding in a year in a half, is taking place at White Space Lab (In japan). "次回9/25金　未来都市ZUYORはゲストにzyganiさん、T4ichiさん、そして1年半ぶりにNekuraさんをお迎えします　場所は今回もWhiteSpaceLabですが、前回同様予約制にする予定です(配信もあるのでご安心を)　予約フォームは本日22:00に解禁します、お見逃しなく! "

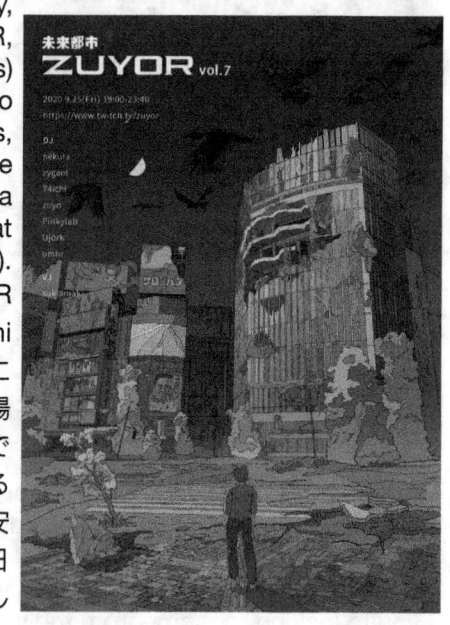

# & NEW NOTEWORTHY

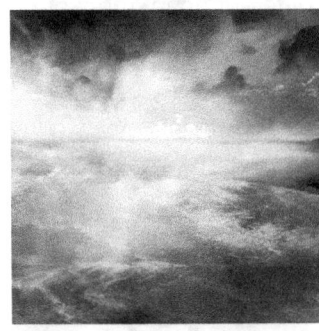

### Voyage / Embrace by 2814

2814 surprised us earlier in the month by releasing a two track dreampunk album on Virtual Dream Plaza. Overall the album as been received quite well, and alot of people begging for a cassette. For some reason Virtual Dream Plaza decided to release a CD instead. Tbh, this is pretty good ambient to meditate to.

### 上海 / 香港 by 沙漠鱿鱼

Speaking of Virtual Dream Plaze, the latest Hiraeth Record 上海 / 香港 was mastered by them. Shanghai / Hong Kong is the brainchild of two well known vaporwave artists, Uncle Squidz and Desert Sand Feel Warm at Night. Typically, I wouldn't have paired the two artists but they totally delivered a wonderful Dreamslush experience. Cassettes, MDs, CD and vinyl are still available.

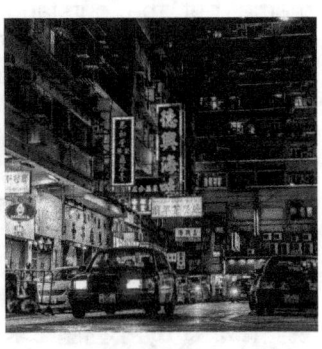

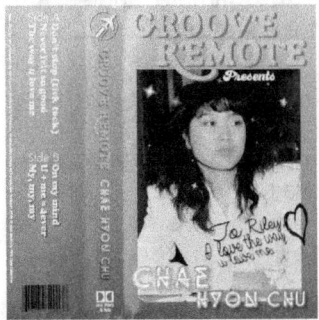

### Chae Hyon Chu by Groove Remote

I passed on this on first release as I thought it was going to be future funk but man was I wrong. Take the best sounds of 90s R&B, vaporize it and throw in some sound effects and you've got some jams. That Tick Tock track is so good. I also love that this is "a private collection of long songs originally intended to be given to that someone special." First Class Collective got a gem on this release.

## 松 by 秋

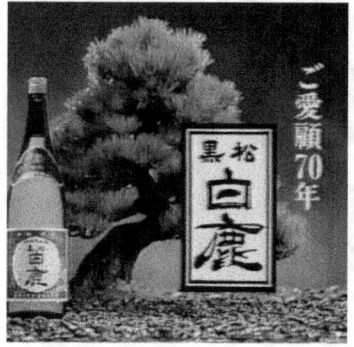

This is almost like signalwave CMs but none of the vocals. So take that idea put it into a 40 minute mix and you've got some great background music. The album cover looks completely different than the actual experience, yet it fits so well after listening. I really enjoyed track 1 at 14:00, reminds me of GT2.

## Warehouse no. 1 by Forklift Operator *(favorite album of Sept)*

I don't know if this album was intentionally trying to come off as a meme but the outstanding oriental music says otherwise. Close your eyes, sit on your forklift and listen to the silent woods with this one. As the sun shines and occasionally provides you with warmth, a butterfly lands on your shoulder, you've escape from your 9-5. You'll be alright.

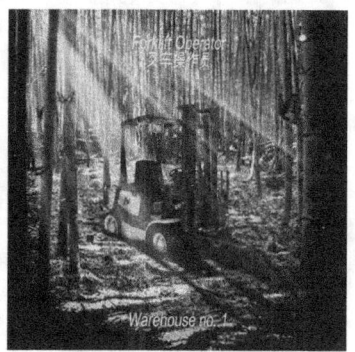

## 現実になる by 不動産マネージャー

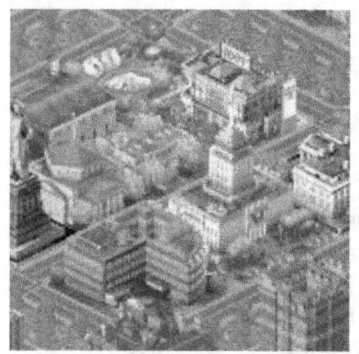

I miss early PC world building games. How simple the camera angles are, the wonderful pixel art, the economy one could build and the city that represented one's own mind. This is what this album gives back to me. A childhood, on outdated technology but stands the test of time.
It isn't your typical sims music, more orchestrated, relaxing Sunday morning vibes.

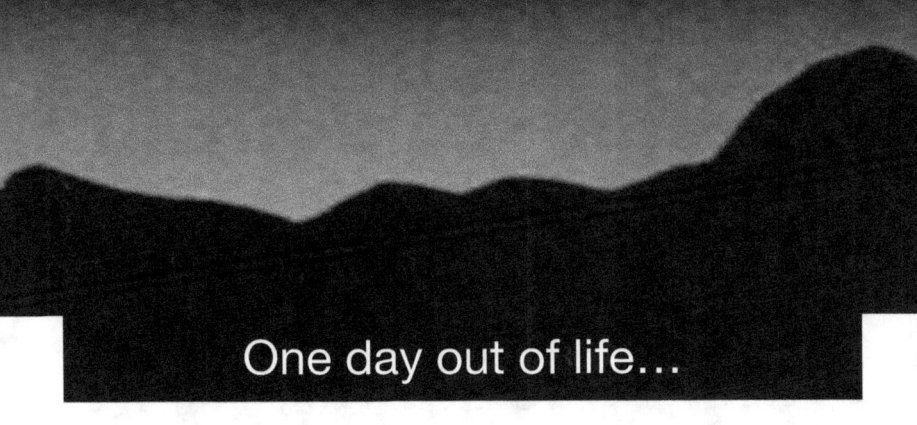

# One day out of life...

Once upon the memories of childhood experiences, you find yourself in the dank barely lit basement rummaging through a box of old VHS and cassettes that look familiar. You can almost taste the bitter sorrow as you wish you still had an analog player to relive the memories. Letting a part of your childhood sit in a box, abandoned would be a crime. Carrying the box up the stairs and through your kitchen your mom notices and asks what inside? Just some old childhood things you throw out as you continue to your room. You wonder if she ever had a childhood as she boils pasta for dinner.

You dump the box on your bed and to your surprise you find an old red cassette player. You open the back up to accidentally breaking the battery cover, of course inside is a crusty leaked battery. After 10 minutes of cleaning it out with alcohol, you are ready to test your first cassette. Fresh batteries in, you wonder what you should listen to first. Looking over your collection, you decide on a favorite, Madonna *The Immaculate Collection*. Holiday starts to play but you notice something off... your cassette players belt is weak. *Hoooolliiidaaay*. Then it randomly speeds up, *celibrate*!

You've discovered something important but you don't know what. A sound so unique yet different. It's almost inspiring.. but then your mom calls you down for dinner. You throw the player on your bed, leaving your room. Little did you know it would be the last time the player would ever work. Who wants music like this, anyways...

# ◢ bandcamp
## TOP RELEASES

1. Promise of Summer by Tsudio Studio (feat. HALLCA)
2. Warehouse no. 1 by Forklift Operator
3. 上海 / 香港 by 沙漠魷魚
4. Planeta by Tiempo para Pensar
5. deep dark trench bside by christ†††
6. 夢の庭園 by Glaciology
7. atlantic memories by vcr-classique
8. 松 by 秋
9. 癒されない傷跡 by prgm。人形
10. 【Ｌｏｓｔ＿Ｓｏｕｌｓ】 by 超高 Titan
11. 絶望に負けた by Macroblank
12. 東京予想 by MAX天気
13. GentleMann by NeverMann
14. Goodbye Future Funk by CHANCE デラソウル
15. Tales from Machine City: Exterminating Angels by vid.nas
16. Reload! by Z.E.R.O
17. ネオン迷宮での生活 LIFƎ IN THƎ NƎΘN LΛBYRINTH by 生涯 Memory Index™
18. Waves by Division Street
19. Smile In The Rain - EP by サクラ SAKURA-LEE
20. bestmott by baemott
21. julia [single] by eccodroid
22. 内部を見る Vol. 2 by INTERFACE マスターストライカー
23. Destination Spa by DATAGIRL
24. 週末アドベンチャー ep by super nintendo
25. Gateway by Soul▲Craft
26. Transparency by MISE
27. the truth is out there by Woah Fuckin Alien
28. 音楽を遅くする by 蒸気ＳＯＵＲＣＥ
29. Inspired Dreams of Promising Futures by Ｄ３４ＤＩＮ５ＩＤ３
30. いつも素敵が隣にいる。 by Lifelines
31. CALI GOLD by
32. MONOSCOPIC
33. 金曜日の夜 by インターネット
34. ﾑﾚWﾑﾘ丐 ﾚの刀ﾓﾚﾘ by Matheus Felipe
35. 永遠の思い出 by Tokyo3018 & SCP2007
36. 放棄された(Abandoned) by Jaded Luxuries
37. 松 by 秋
38. Panorama Cotton by headroom
39. 再生 by 夜間視力NIGHT VISION.Corp
40. ミニジャーニー1：月光 by エーテ ルMALLS
41. 幻 by 棺
42. Dance by Cd Rom Palm
43. トルコスペシャル by ＳＵＰＥＲＬ ＵＣＥＮＴ 超明るい
44. Designer Dreams by Amadeus Vegas
45. Vice Vibes 2 by Hatebot
46. Magic Moments by PJS
47. Sleepless Nights by Lord Fiji
48. ＳＵＰＥＲＬＵＣＥＮＴ－ＣＲＥＳＴＡ
49. Alligatum by ＡＸＩＯＭＡ～１１ ２３ (right)
50. Emotional EP by Machina Pensant
51. 나는 다음에 무슨 일이 일어날 지 모른 다 by From Tokyo to Honolulu
52. Warehouse no. 1 by Forklift Operator
53. 現実になる by 不動産マネー ジャー
54. A Material Life by Crisii
55. お天気チャンネル / weather channel thingies by ＳＵＰＥＲＬＵ ＣＥＮＴ 超明るい
56. **BALLADS FOR: THE BENEVOLENT** by Ｇａｎｇｊｉｒａ
57. Vendredi by CANAL+
58. Palm Island by TIMEWAVEZER0
59. FANTASY by KNGHT

# PITCH SHIFTER
## ONE YEAR LATER

クリスタル**KITSUNE:** *"Ever since I was little I wanted to go to Japan. To be honest, it blew my mind how amazing my first trip trip was and I was able to spend every second with my friends! The images that are engrained in my head will forever be there. Walking down the back streets of Tokyo or listening to music on our phones at the park at 12 in the morning. Ordering sushi only to find out it was a take-away order so we had to figure out where to eat this big box of sushi we now own. Walking down that one extra street just to explore. Every second was a story, but we were living that story. We were the ones making everything happen. Playing a show in Japan on the other hand is something I, never in a million years, thought I would have been able to do. After spending a week meeting and making new friends, I had the chance to perform with them. Showing up in Shibuya after a train ride with pounds DJ equipment in our hands and on our back's, everyone was nervous. But as soon as we saw that venue sign and taking a trip under the ground, we knew this was going to be amazing! Finally being able to put faces with names we got ready to play a show of a lifetime, and it truly was. Coming up above ground and seeing the morning sunlight after playing a show underground for the past 6 or so hours was kind of breathtaking in a way. I'm so glad I had my camera with me the entire trip, even if I can still visualize every moment of the trip, I'm glad I'll always have something to look back on in a sentimental way. I couldn't have picked a better crew of people to explore the city with and I'd really like to give my heartfelt thank you to everyone I met along the way, every Producer, every DJ and every Fan. We know this scene is truly alive; were living in it and making it the best it can be. I'll never give it up for anything~"*

**ΛDRIΛNWΛVE:** *"Japan is fucking awesome. I ate ramen for a week but hey, we're here* for a good time, not a long time.

"This country is extra special in my head for countless reasons, most notably that no matter where you are in Tokyo, there is a 100% chance you will accidentally end up in a porn shop at least once, much to KITE0080's dismay. No complaints here, though (I, uh, may or may not have purchased some hentai manga & forgot the bag in a konbini).

The Japanese Future Funk scene is very alive, & we loved every moment of the PITCH SHIFTER show Kissmenerdygirl put together. It was really cool to chill with all the other artists, & the energy from the crowd was almost too much for the venue to hold. The クリスタル KITSUNE x ΛDRIΛNWΛVE collab track reveal was a lot of fun too! I gave the owner an extra ΛDRIΛNWΛVE t-shirt as thanks & he was like "Hold on," and handed me one of HIS t-shirts! Hopefully next time I can cash in the free drink voucher I brought back to America on accident."

**Sparkly Night:** "Walking down the streets of Tokyo wearing just the shorts and a pair of slides (because it was still super hot even in September) was something that will stay in my mind for a long time. Together with クリスタルKITSUNE, KITE0080 and ΛDRIΛNWΛVE we had the greatest time buying a shit ton of soda in every vending machine we could find.

Living this life with my friends from the Future Funk and Vaporwave scene really did seem unreal and dreamy at the time. Words can't express what I felt then and what I feel now, a year later, looking at the pictures we took, but I know for sure that it was genuinely magical.

I stayed in Japan for 4 months (had my ups and downs) but I think the time that I spent with my friends was the most fun.

One time in Akihabara, we went to the porn shop and KITE0080 wouldn't go with me to the top floor, the "forbidden" one, because he was too embarassed.

Tons of porn sorted alphabetically by categories and older guys walking around, checking out the back of the DVDs.

There was a clerk behind the cabin which covered everything but his hands so he could stay anonymous.

Sounds like a decent job.

Love y'all!"

**KITE0080:** "Hanging out with the boys was way better than I expected. It was my first time traveling abroad to literally live with some people for an extended period of time. We got an AirBnb in a small residential area which we slowly adventured out into. Between Kitsune and myself, we practically lived off 711 food. I think I ate sushi and had some 100円 drink every single day. It was the life because we were eating good and on a small budget. Speaking of which, for some crazy reason we went into a small family owned (im guessing) bar restaurant and shared a plate of food, I think all 4 of us. Why were we so cheap? I guess at the time I didn't have a job but I remember every day we'd fight over food. So when we finally decided 711 and this small grocery store was our two locations, tensions fell. I think the biggest meal e ate was this 100+ plate of sushi that confusingly were able to get as take out. I knew a small park near by (which was really a 20 minute walk probably) and we ate on this bench under a small amount of light. A bunch of foreigners eating sushi and being merry in a residential area, it was the dream. Sparkly Night taught us how to make a kimchi tofu dish, Andrianwave seemed to always be vaping and Kitsune was making Future Funk jams. Living together was awesome, and almost feels like a dream. I'm so grateful we had the chance before covid. Who knew."

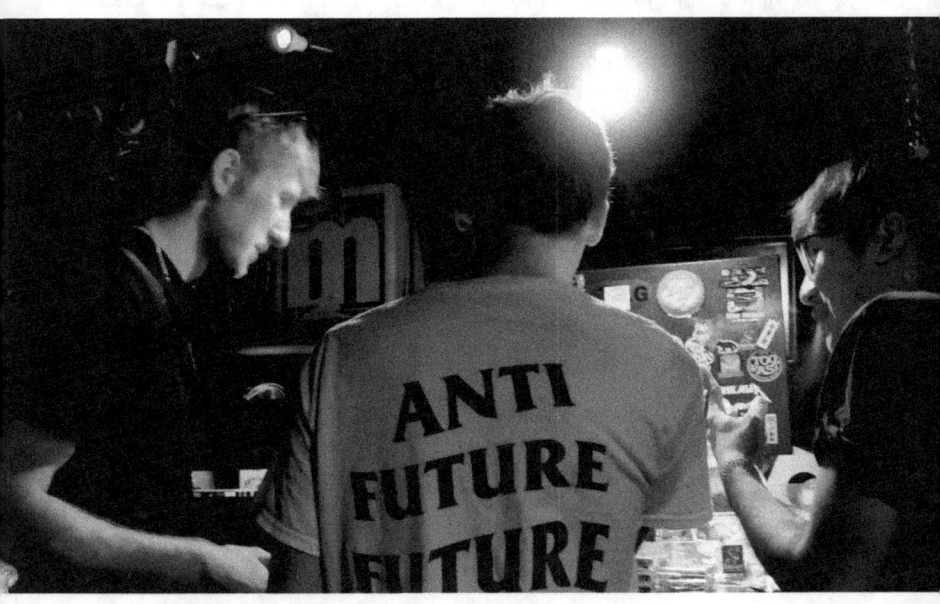

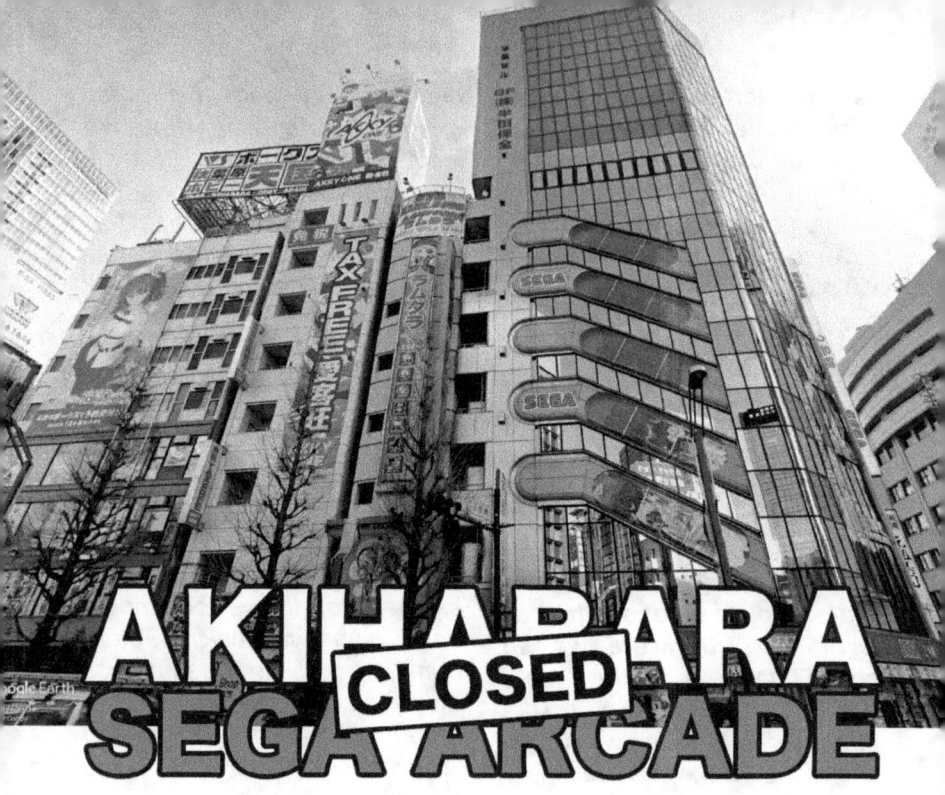

# AKIHABARA
## CLOSED
## SEGA ARCADE

Nothing worse than hearing about a location you'll never get to visit closing down. After 17 years, the SEGA arcade massive skyscraper as announced its closing. Inside the building countless japanese video games, anime and more have been part of the history of this Akihabara location. Some even credit this location as the cause for the incredible boom of the otaku culture in the early 2000s.

I don't remember if I had passed or even went into this building as I do remember seeing a SEGA building but photos of this don't look too familiar. Regardless, it's a stable in the culture and it's sad to see it go.

They didn't announce why it was closing but some speculate it's due to covid. Which brings up a good point, crowded places like Akihabara (which is practically elbow to elbow) will never be the same. At least not for a long time. Let's hope this isn't a sign of how other cultural staples are heading. I suppose after covid, take every chance you can to visit the places you want to see.

# 佐藤博 HIROSHI SATOH THIS BOY

## CITY POP HISTORY

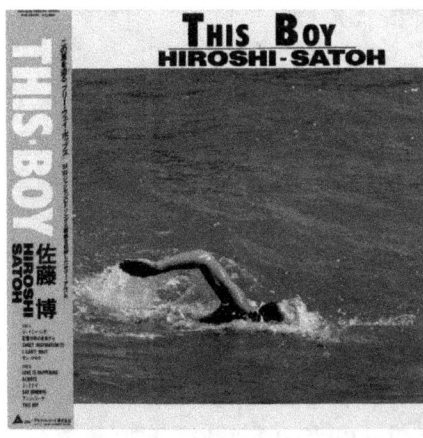

Japanese City pop is thriving in this 1985 masterpiece. This Boy is one of the most requested repressing releases from the gold age of city pop and yet some how no one has been able to get it done. With an average price of 150 USD, you're more likely to listen to this one on Youtube.

The entire album is a wonderful mix and classic City pop, with MOOG sytnhs, electronic drums and a voice that soothes the soul.

With the track, "Say Goodbye" being the most popular from the release, it'll have to thinking on past relationships both ones you left or they left you; "I'm gone Though you tried to own me I guess there's no harm done Hope you won't be lonely". The hook, "Say goodbye" is too good and I guess hope, we all won't always be lonely~

---

## English Album Tracks:

| | | | | |
|---|---|---|---|---|
| A1 | Shiny Lady | | B2 | Always |
| A2 | Kioku No Naka No Mirai Kara | | B3 | Gemini |
| A3 | Sweet Inspiration '85 | | B4 | Say Goodbye |
| A4 | I Can't Wait | | B5 | Angelina |
| A5 | Sun Glow | | B6 | This Boy |
| B1 | Love Is Happening | | | |

# BEHIND THE NAME

## Ursula's Cartridges // @UrsulasCartri

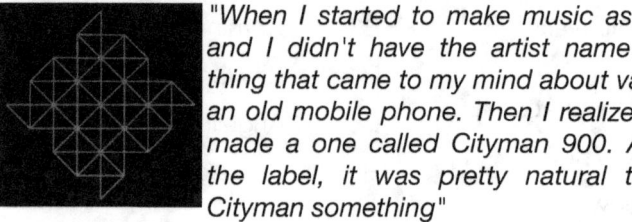

*"I like the word "cartridge". I like it how it sounds in English. Also, i remember that there was an alphabet poster in our English class back in the third grade and each alphabet had their specific names for English people. U had Ursula so it kind of stayed in my mind for years plus it's an "exotic" sounding name. Also, it's a very uncommon name these days.* And no, it has nothing to do with the baddie from Disney's Little Mermaid. I actually realized it afterwards that there's the mean octopus lady in a Disney movie. :D

Also, the name also reminds me of Jane's Addiction. I don't seem to know any other music artist nor band to have a similar "Something's something" type of a name"

## *b l u e s c r e e n* // @TylerEllis18

*"My name comes from the dreaded blue screen of death, but also blue as I'm sad, a nod to my depression.*

*I think if I can remind people about the mental health dialogue, even if its hidden behind a double meaning, or obscured, then it's better than just having a name that sounds cool."*

## Cityman Productions // @cityman900

*"When I started to make music as Cityman 900 and I didn't have the artist name yet, the first thing that came to my mind about vaporwave was an old mobile phone. Then I realized that Mobira made a one called Cityman 900. After I started the label, it was pretty natural to just call it Cityman something"*

### [PATRYK FILMS] // @Ludamage

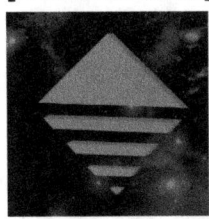

"As I'm spending the time at the job's workplace 8 hours everyday where played radio all the time i tried my first single "forbidden skin/motive" as a DJing on switching the radio channels in real time. That was so awkward and raw try i don't really liked and thought never do anything under it, but in 2012 December comes The Needle Drop video about Mac Plus review and all things i knew early came up to me in one piece - to produce vaporwave as soon as possible till it's a fresh move in style i ever dreamed to participate into but didn't know how yet. Thats why i used the such alias name after my first Slander Fall project which was way originally made out of FL instruments and used not much samples at all as the WTF after.

TMTЧM is mostly like a russian opposite of how WTFFM stands for, but in a lil changed meaning

Laserprint Tech. is sort of a company that stands behind the main plot for a first album Reality Net

Vitsballkona is a slowest ambienty vapor, which has a split of the words Vit (from russian Vid - view), s (russian S - from), ballkona (russian balkon - balcony)"


### Fujifire // @fujifiremusic

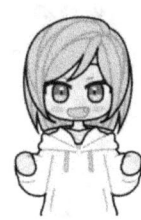

"I first came up with name about 5 years ago before I even loved anime, when I was thinking of Starfire from teen titans and a Japanese buffet that was called Fuji buffet. That's how I first thought of the name Fujifire but it wasn't my music name until January 2018."


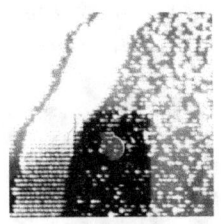

⟨👆⟩ タンジェリン // @KagoTangerine

"👆👆👆👆👆👆👆👆👆！！！"

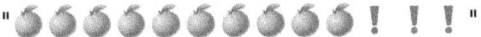

## NATIONAL ナショナル // @FM_NATIONAL_

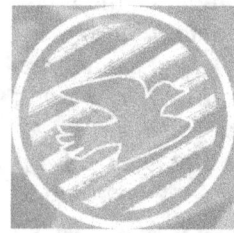

*"The origin of my artist name came from an electronic device that have the name 'national' on it. I put Japanese translation at the back because most of the artist in 2015-2016 period put Japanese words on their names and releases."*

## Seikomart // @Seikomartjapan

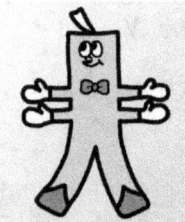

*"The most popular and famous local convenience store that originated in Hokkaido actually exists under the name "Seicomart".*
*We wanted to become a community-based label like this convenience store on the internet. Then it became konbini "Seikomart"!"*

## FAT MAN MIAMI // @fatmanmiami

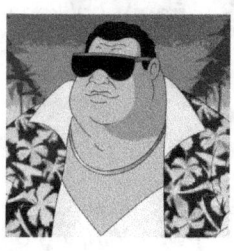

*"It was a joke with a friend of mine while playing Team Fortress 2. I made the heavy character look real wave-y by equipping a hawaiian shirt and I came up with renaming the shirt item to «Fat Man Miami». Then I got an idea of using that name for mu vaporwave project. My friend (who also does my artwork) was a little unsure at first of me using it as an actual artist name, but I ended up with that ha."*

## aquablanca // @aquablanca2

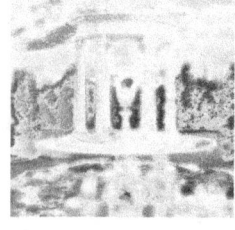

*"AB is a nostalgic place that is very special to the creator. It brings memories of a place they have dreamed of many times, but never actually went to."*

# [PATRYK FILMS]
## CURRENT PHYSICAL RELEASES FOR ALL HIS PROJECTS

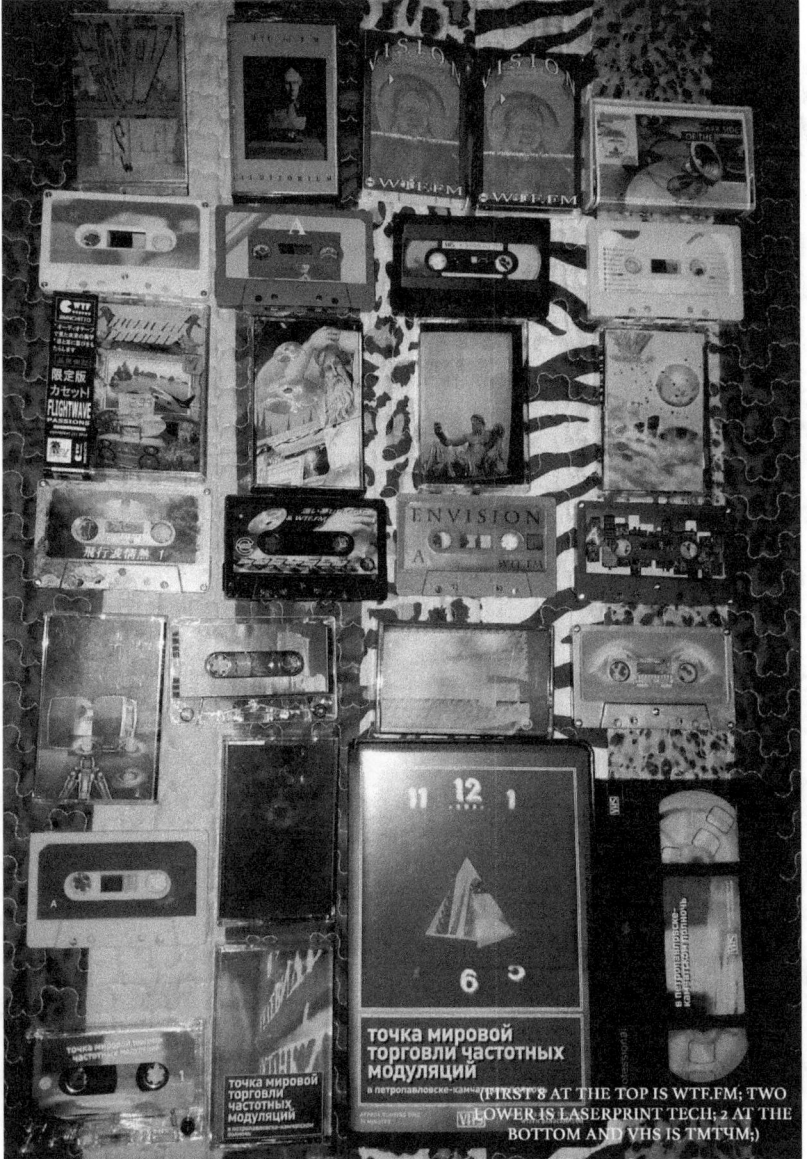

точка мировой
торговли частотных
модуляций

(FIRST 8 AT THE TOP IS WTF.FM; TWO
LOWER IS LASERPRINT TECH; 2 AT THE
BOTTOM AND VHS IS TMTЧМ;)

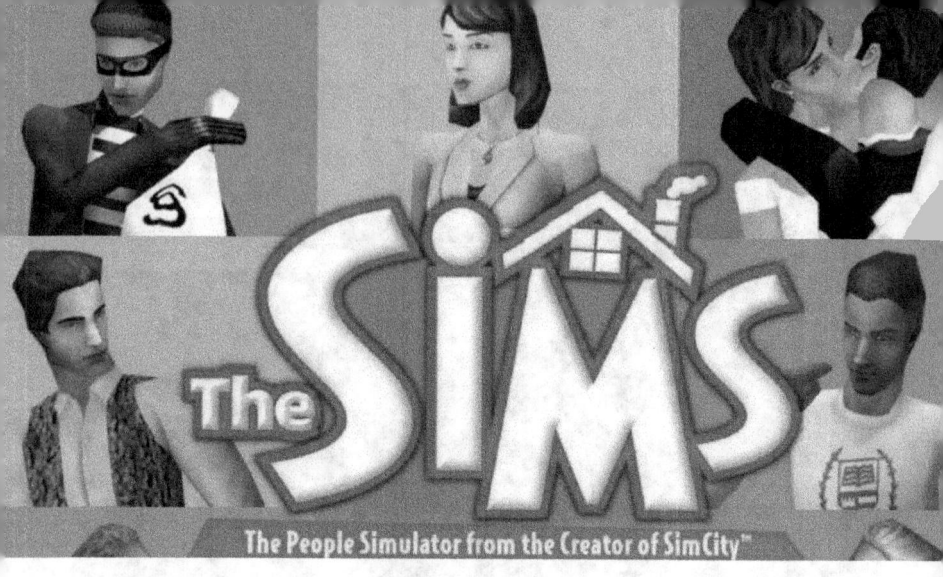

# The Sims, Original - PC Cheats

Press CTRL+SHIFT+C during game to display the command prompt. Then enter any of the following:

- **Klapaucius** – 1000 Simoleons
- **water_tool** – Island home
- **hist_add** – Add new family history to family
- **auto_level** – Architecture tools automatically set the level as needed
- **house <house number>** – Automatically load indicated house, no questions asked
- **prepare_lot** – Check and fix required lot objects
- **edit_char** – Create-a-character mode
- **Interests** – Display personality and interests
- **draw_all_frames** off – Draw all animation frames disabled
- **draw_all_frames** on – Draw all animation frames enabled
- **draw_origins** – Draw colored dots at each person's origin
- **sim_log** end – End sim logging
- **draw_floorable** off – Floorable grid disabled
- **draw_floorable** on – Floorable grid enabled
- **map_edit off** – Map editor disabled
- **map_edit on** – Map editor enabled
- **move_objects** – Move any object
- **rotation <0-3>** – Rotate camera
- **autonomy <1-100>** – Set free thinking level
- **reload_people** – Total reload of people skeletons, animations, suits and skins

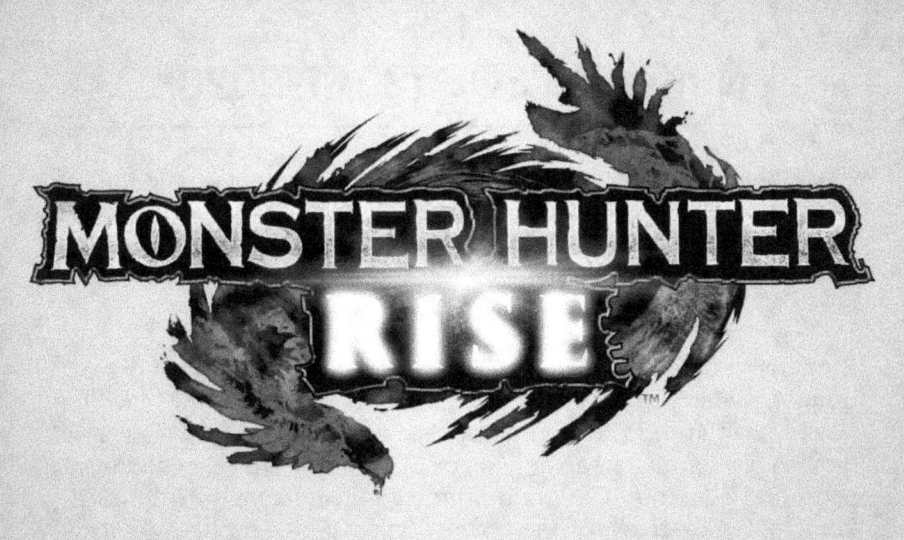

# Monster Hunter Rise Announced!

Nintendo earlier in Sept had a Nintendo Direct Mini and the game that took the center stage had to be Monster Hunter Rise. They even had an extra 15 minute segment showing off the new combat, monsters and environments.

The rise in this title is related to new ways to moving around the maps. For the first time, we have a wolf/dog vehicle that allows for quicker track up and down the map. They are calling these canines "Palamute", which has unlimited speed and help during battles. Obviously your cat pals are still part of your support and during main campaign you can have two while multiplayer a single cat.

The "flagship" monster for this game is called a "Magnamalo" which is a fanged wyvern. The purple glowing energy and mean mug makes this boss look really cool. They added a couple new monsters but this one looks the coolest.

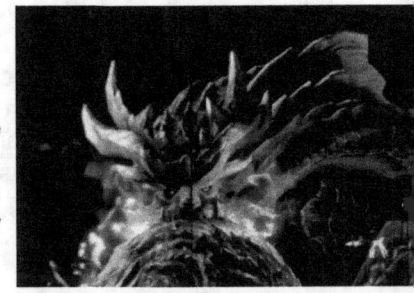

I've been a fan of the series since the PSP days and once I get a switch, this will be a day one buy for me. (oh MHS2 was announced directly after!!!!)

# Nintendo 3DS (2011-2020)

The same day as mini-direct, Nintendo also announced the end of the Nintendo 3DS life-cycle. From 2011 to 2020, it had a great 9 year run but it was obvious once the handheld capabilities of the Nintendo Switch was announced, the 3DS life was coming to an end.

Strangely enough, the New 3DS was my last console/handheld I bought. When Game Freak announced a remake of my favorite Pokemon game, Pokemon Ruby, I knew I had to get back into gaming. I bought a steak gray/black 3DS used from eBay and went head first into the 3DS world. Throughout my loyalty to the 3DS fandom I owned every Pokemon games, Fire Emblem, Fantasy Life, and so much more but the game I spent the most time with was Terraria.

Now normally, big Terraria fans you'll meet instantly can tell you about the latest and greatest updates and gameplay from the PC version. The NDS version barely received any updates and for the most part got stuck at Desktop equivalent of 1.2.1 but that didn't matter. At that point Terraria had such much content packed into this small cart that even to this day I don't feel like I've actually explore more than 50% of the game. I'm not a PC gamer, I'm a macOS programmer, so I never really had the desire or the excitement people share in the Minecraft world but Terraria was my minecraft. I spent hours and hours building complex homes and structures, upgrading to the most powerful weapons and gear and building the most sporadic tunneling systems known to made. And I loved every minute of it.

After I turned 27, I put down my 3DS for the last time and started to focus on MTHU and started to feel guilty spending time doing anything else but working on MTHU. Even after the amazing announcement of the Switch, I hadn't gotten into gaming at all. I just don't have the time or need to breakaway from the real world. So although the N3DS wasn't my childhood device, it surely had an impact on me for 7 years and it made my early 20s a real adventure. It'll be sad to see you go but thank you for the memories.

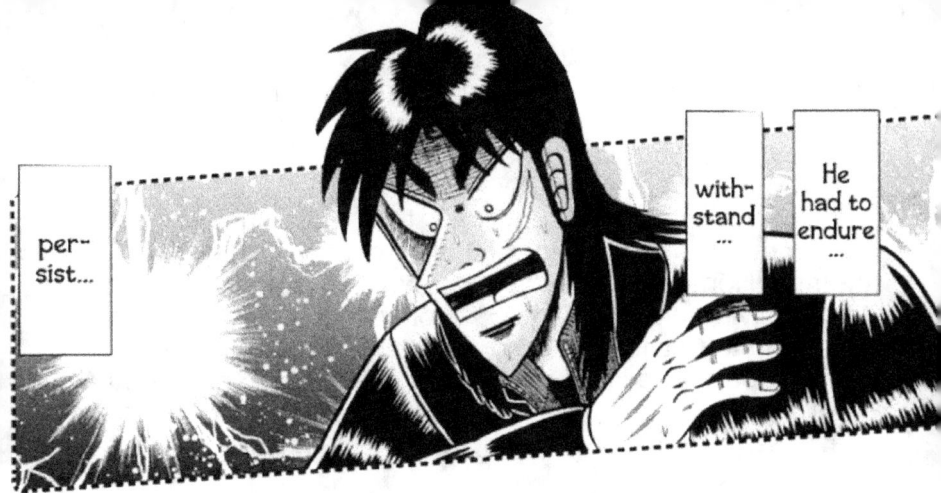

# 賭博黙示録カイジ

賭博黙示録カイジ or *tobaku datenroku kaiji*, was recommended to me after I finished reading the Manga, Homunculus. Both are apparently dive deep into the psychology of the main character and pushing the reader to the limits of their own experience. Before reading Kaiji, the only impress I had was a character ready to sacrifice anything to win a bet. I mean the cover said, "The Gamble of Demons.." But that's on Chapter 256: 2.4 billion which online seems to be the start of the English translations, just an fyi.

The manga starts with Kaiji and his two partners in crime stealing 2 billion after apparently forcefully winning a poker match. They are required to escape the facility in which 10 suitcases contains their winnings. It's kind of comical to see how they manage a roof top chair throwing each suitcase in front of them or up ladders to finally find/steal a small flatbed truck. At this point, I'm getting a lot of Lupin the 3rd vibes just with a sharper edged manga style. This definitely does not have the psychological horror feel Homunculus has.

Behind a garage door, the 3 pray to their gods that the open road awaits them. Unfortunately, the black suits are waiting for them so so a new chase begins and some how everyone knows our runaways by name. Circling the premises, there is no way out but a small gap between a car, a Black Suit and some shrubs. Kaiji pleads with the driver to, "Just this once", floor it and run over the guard. The driver really isn't having it and starts to cry. I'm starting to think this crew of misfits are just kind hearted dudes who like stealing from the rich.

I won't spoil their escape but they now face a bigger challenge. The money is foreign and they are in a foreign country. None of them have their passports and must return to their living arrangements, "... only once you do that, that you can start calling that money yours", Kaiji explains. From the passports, we learn one of them is Chinese and the other from the Philippines. If the Black Suites get their hands on the passports first, everything they've achieved thus far is pointless.

We get a hint that the crew was betrayed by an ex-roommate and that the Black Suits were actually torturing the crew into gambling. Regardless, they get their passports with their money in hand. I thought for sure Kaiji was going to some how lose his two other crew mates but they actually all seem like friends. There is something quite peculiar about the last hand of poker played. "It was outrageous", "It was impossible" and Kaiji felt the exact same way. Kaiji was even betting on all three of their lives, had he lost... well he didn't and somewhere deep inside, he knew he wouldn't because he raised his opponent. But what really was Kaiji's reason for being able to take the risk?

I don't want to review the entire manga obviously, but I like the vibe I'm getting off so far. It's not very serious, the characters seem like old chums but for some reason, it doesn't feel like there's much risk. They either escape back to their home countries, or get caught. What's on the line if Kaiji is already willing to bet their lives? Find out for yourself, in Chapter 7: Expatiation.

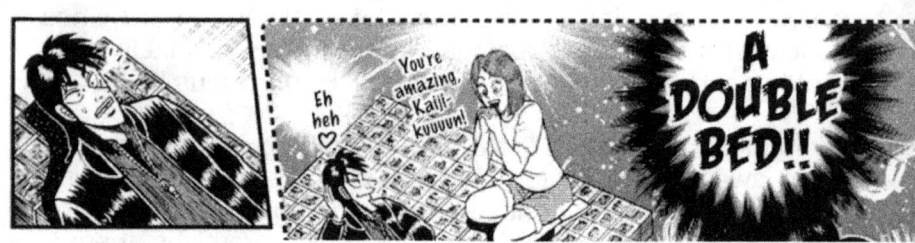

# 学习中文
## LEARN CHINESE

It's time we learn some real words. Something from some daily life. HSK 1 is great for the first 100 words but you'll never be able speak about Vaporwave. So let's learn some *aesthetic* words:

| | | |
|---|---|---|
| 安装 | ān zhuāng | install |
| 软体 | ruǎn tǐ | software |
| 网页 | wǎng yè | web page |
| 晶体 | jīng tǐ | crystal |
| 宫殿 | gōng diàn | palace |
| 作业系统 | zuò yè xì tǒng | OS |
| 生意 | shēng yi | business |
| 音乐 | yīn yuè | Music |
| 广播 | guǎng bō | broadcast |
| 媒体 | méi tǐ | Media |
| 厚 | hòu | Thick |
| 计划 | jì huà | project |
| 视讯 | shì xùn | video call |
| 能源 | néng yuán | energy |
| 口罩 | kǒu zhào | Face mask |
| 视窗 | Shì chuāng | Windows OS |
| 蒸气波 | zhēng qì Bō | Vaporwave |
| 山下达郎 | Shānxià dá láng | Tatsuro Yamashita |

# 5 HORROR-THEMED ALBUMS FOR HALLOWEEN

By Jay Wallace

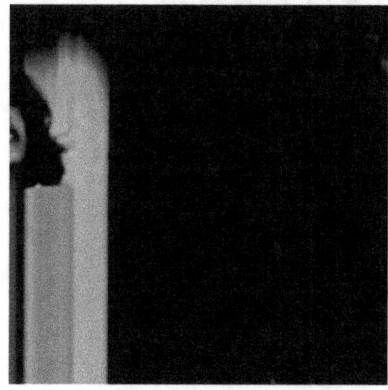

### Hallowave by EPX90

Released in September on Origami-Vato's Bandcamp page, this Vaporgoth/Signalwave album is a dark celebration of All Hallow's Eve. Not content to use just horror movie clips, Hallowave recreates a Halloween evening in front of the TV with late night movies ("Midnight Movie") and evening news warnings of the past. ("Candy Apples and Razor Blades")

### spook by m a l i b l u e : (

Featuring a warped image of a terrified Jamie Lee Curtis, m a l i b l u e's spook samples classic horror films like Blair Witch Project, Christine, and Friday The 13th and layers them over nerve-racking drones, aggressive synths and drums, and samples of forgotten pop hits. One of the best Vapordrone albums out there, and the best to listen to on Halloween night.

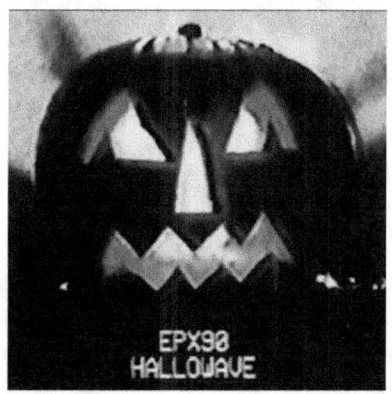

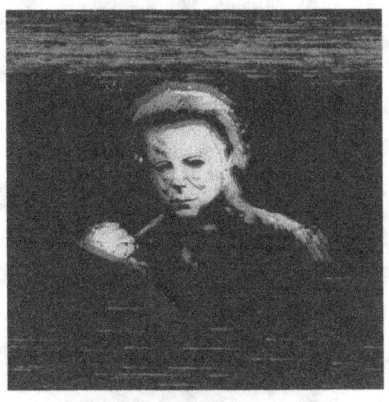

## Empty Shapes by The Reaver Crowley

Using only clips of John Carpenter's Halloween, The Reaver Crowley has crafted the perfect love letter to the seminal slasher film, capturing the unease of watching Michael Myers – a.k.a The Shape – stalk the friends of Laurie Strode.

## STALKER by STALKER *(below)*

Available on Evening Disclosure, S T A L K E R is a Dark Ambient Signalwave album with only five tracks of droning terror: "Figure," "Shape," Pale," "Hunt," and "Prey." It's simple, to the point, and makes the hairs on your neck stand up. Though maybe not like our next entry…

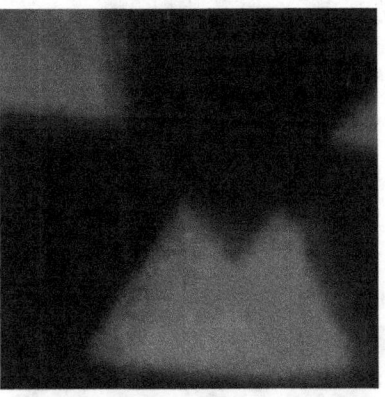

## Family Dinner by Necrilla *(left)*

Another release from Evening Disclosure, Necrilla's Family Dinner is a Gore Ambient Signalwave album. Yes, "Gore Ambient." I won't evening try to describe this, so I'll leave you with the four-word album description: "nothing beats moms cooking!…"

But wait there's more…

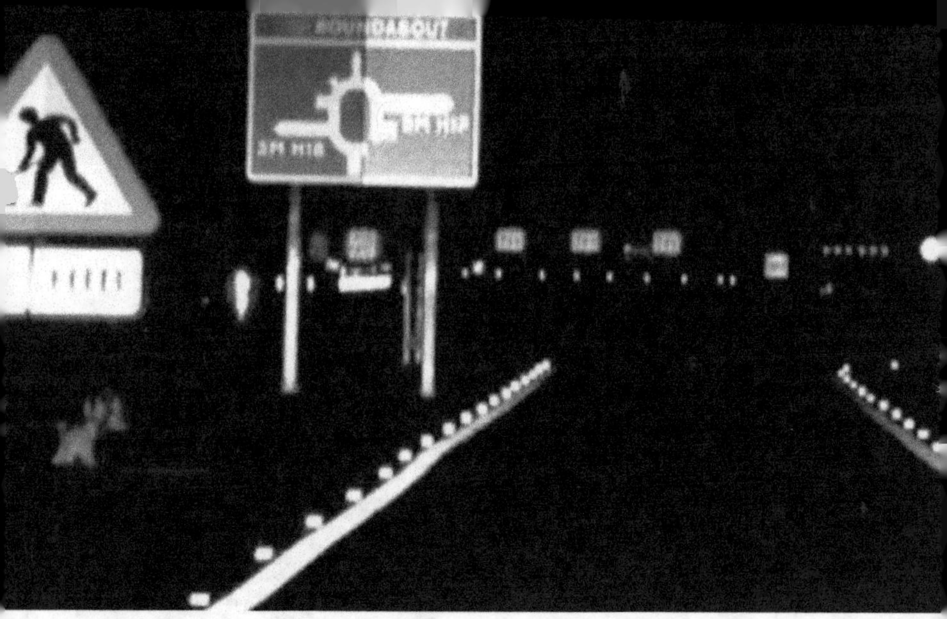

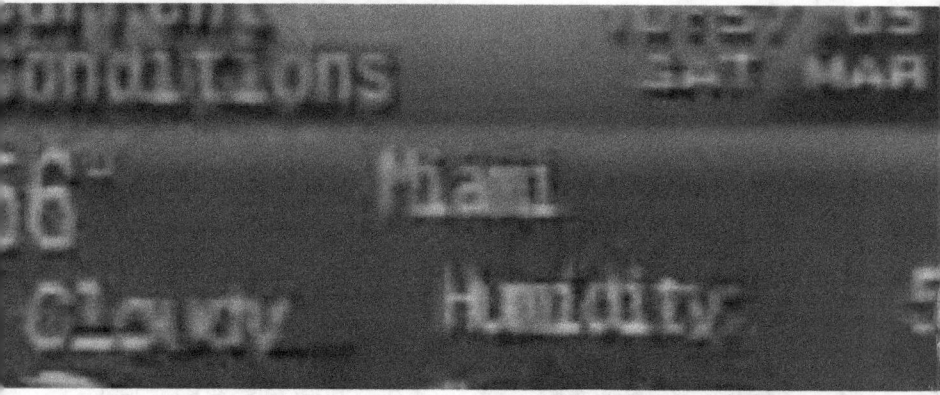

## Highway of Blood by TVVIN_PINEZ_M4LL & CH03

Two unconventional albums for you. First, a two track collaboration using mid-century rock tracks and 1960s-era driver safety scare films. A real lo-fi oddity.

## WEATHER FORCAST 2033 by FUTURE WEATHER CHANNEL

Finally, a Cursed Climatewave from Night Coverage, taking place in the future where we realized too late that climate change is real. How timely!

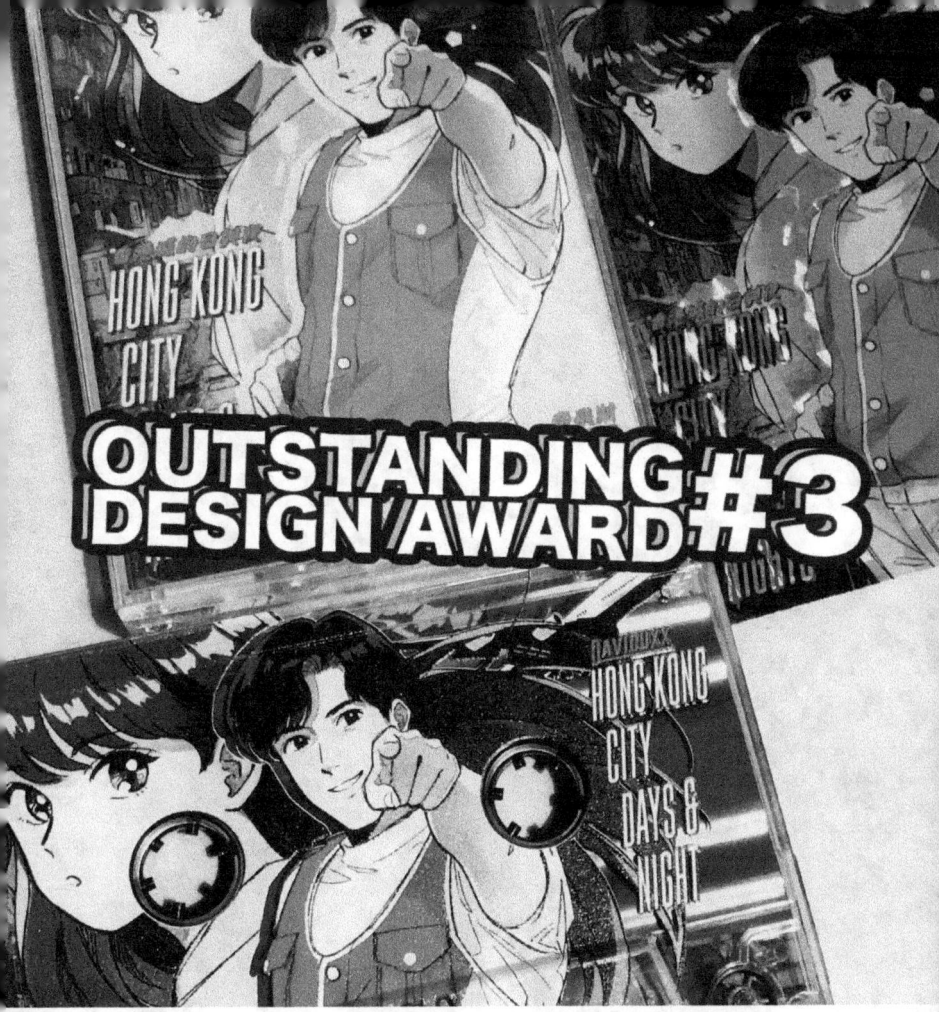

**Hong Kong City Days & Nights by Daviouxx**

When it comes to quality design, Neoncity Records always delivers and there is no exception with Hong City Days & Nights by Daviouxx. From the late 90s anime style to the hong city life in the background to the beautiful screen printed cassette and the additional holographic card that was sent with it, this release is pure eye candy. If that wasn't enough, the music that comes along takes you back to the hong kong dance floor.

Making this release, the Recipient of the **3rd MTHU Outstanding Design Award**

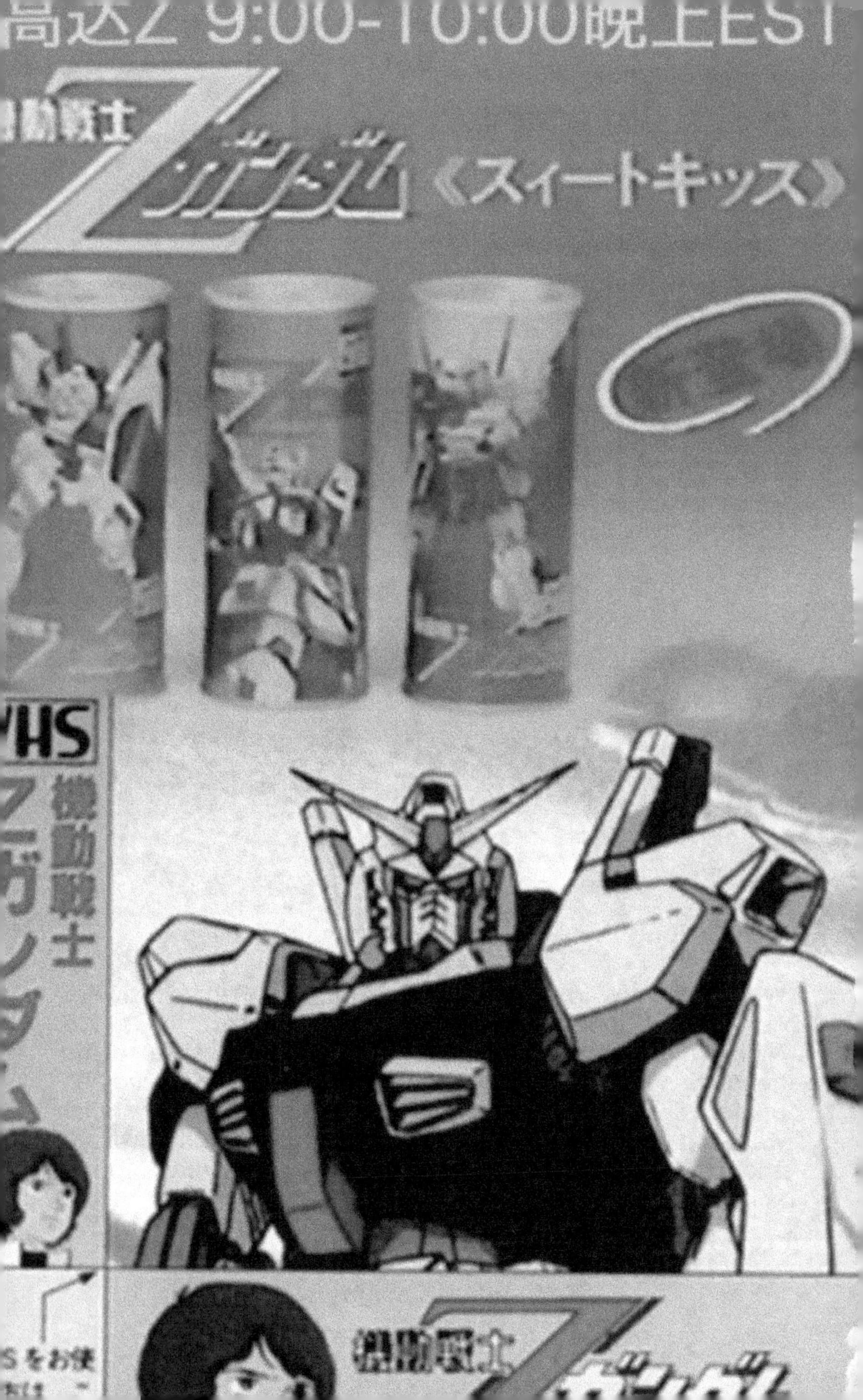

When you're listening to music or even releasing music, a track has a few keywords that describe the release. For example, you just did this sick edit of a EDM track and you're throwing in there BOOTLEG to sound cool and attract more ears, do you even know what bootleg even means? What about REMIX? Did you know there's an unspoken standard for when to use these words? Let's look at some of the most popular:

### Remix
Probably the most used tag, and probably the easiest to understand. A remix is a new mix of a song using the same stems (bass, melody, etc) of the source track. Most likely for it to be an official remix, it will be sanctioned.

### Bootleg
Bootlegs are a little different in the fact that you're remixing using the raw song, ie, sampling the track. It's a bootleg because you didn't get permission to use the sample and you're unofficially releasing.

### VIP
Probably not used as often but a VIP is a remix/boot that takes the song in a completely different direction. Some times this can be seen as *art's name version*. Vaporwave is somewhere in-between a bootleg and VIP release.

### Mashup
Typically this is mixing up multiple songs into a new song. Madeon is the master at this if you haven't heard his track Pop Culture (live mashup) on Youtube.

Regardless, if you even use these is another story. I just was listening to Manicure Records Soundcloud and noticed so many of the tracks use nonsensical remixes or bootlegs and wanted to know what these terms meant.

A. G. Music - Money On A Gold Plate _ Cos I Love U-322897055.mp3
A.G. COOK - HAD 1 (DJ CASHINOUT BOOTLEG EDIT)-155251182.mp3
BOY LIGHTS (JASMINE'S SINGLE TULIP)-149483922.mp3

# Fidde - I Wonder If You Know (Dreams)

Minimalism in EDM, especially house music, grabs me the most. A simple piano stream with a great bass-line and a high hat that keeps it going is difficult to master. Mainly because all three of those layers repeat throughout the entire track with little variance. So how does one keep it interesting? I think from my experience it's the sound levels of percussion and the use of anti sound. If done well, you've got me hooked to your track.

What crave is a track that ultimately hits me with chills. If a house track actually hits me harder than just wanting to dance but think about my life or inspires me, now that is special. So here comes Fidde one day deciding that he found the perfect vocal sample to throw in at the 1:50 mark that changes it all.

"…and i wonder, if you know~ what it means… to find your dreams come true~"

It was intense when that vocal sample hit my ears for the first time. Who isn't reading this right now thinking how badly they wish their dreams would come true already. We're working as hard as we can; releasing music, creating art, uploading YT videos, writing that book, etc, and some how even after it's all done we only incrementally increase or standings in life. How much more do we have to produce to get the recognition we think we deserve?

There's something in that sample, mainly because it sounds like it's from a 60 movie time period piece. Some how like the singer knows the answer and he wants us to gave it for ourselves. I think we can all get it… it just requires time, effort and a lot of energy. If we can keep smashing against that immovable wall it might not move but it might just let us pass through. Oh, how I wonder what it's like to have my dreams come true.

# 9月から10月
## 日本の月間天気

### Average Temperature
**19 September – 18 October**

Probability of below-normal temperature (cold), near-normal temperature (average), above-normal temperature (warm) for each area. Colored areas have a 40% probability or more of below-normal or above-normal temperature.

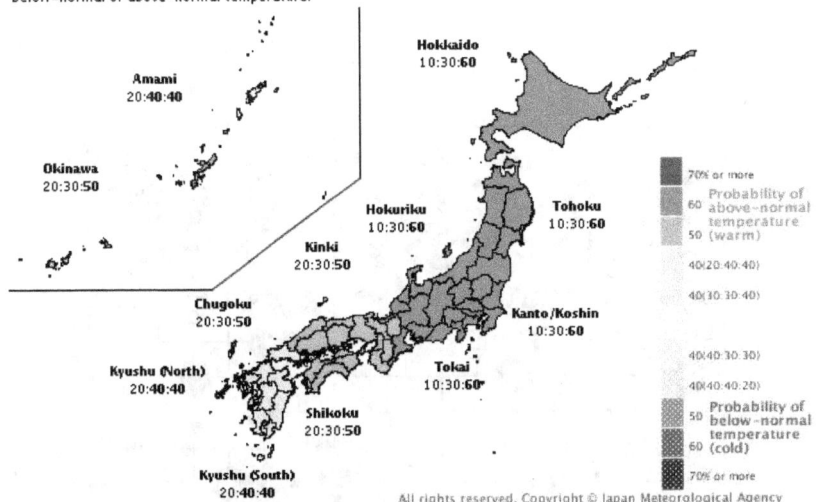

Hokkaido
10:30:60

Amami
20:40:40

Okinawa
20:30:50

Hokuriku
10:30:60

Tohoku
10:30:60

Kinki
20:30:50

Chugoku
20:30:50

Kanto/Koshin
10:30:60

Kyushu (North)
20:40:40

Tokai
10:30:60

Shikoku
20:30:50

Kyushu (South)
20:40:40

| | Probability of above-normal temperature (warm) |
|---|---|
| 70% or more | |
| 60 | |
| 50 | |
| 40(20:40:40) | |
| 40(30:30:40) | |
| 40(40:30:30) | |
| 40(40:40:20) | |
| | Probability of below-normal temperature (cold) |
| 50 | |
| 60 | |
| 70% or more | |

地図上をクリックすると各地方の詳しい予報がご覧いただけます。1か月予報は毎週木曜日14時30分、3か月予報は毎月25日頃14時、暖候期予報は2月、寒候期予報は9月の3か月予報と同時に発表します。このページの予報は、発表時刻から地方毎に順次更新されます。季節予報が発表された地方でも更新されるまでは前回発表の内容が表示されますので、季節予報の内容の確認は、1か月予報は14時40分以降、3か月予報・暖候期予報・寒候期予報は14時10分以降に全国の予報が完全に更新されてからお願いいたします。

One-month and three-month forecasts are issued at 14:30 JST every Thursday and at 14:00 JST around the 25th of each month respectively. Warm- and cold-season outlooks are issued in February and September respectively in concurrence with three-month forecasts.

# 围棋 KAIFU

Date : 2020-09-21
WhitePlayer : Spectral-2d
WhiteRank : 2d
Komi : 7.5

BlackPlayer : K.H.
BlackRank : 28k
Result : W+R

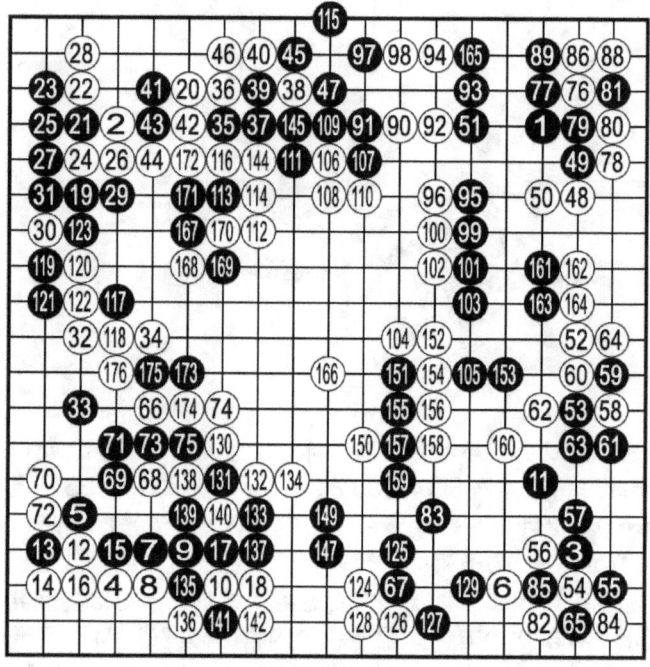

1 - 176

87 at 54    143 at 131    146 at 140    148 at 131

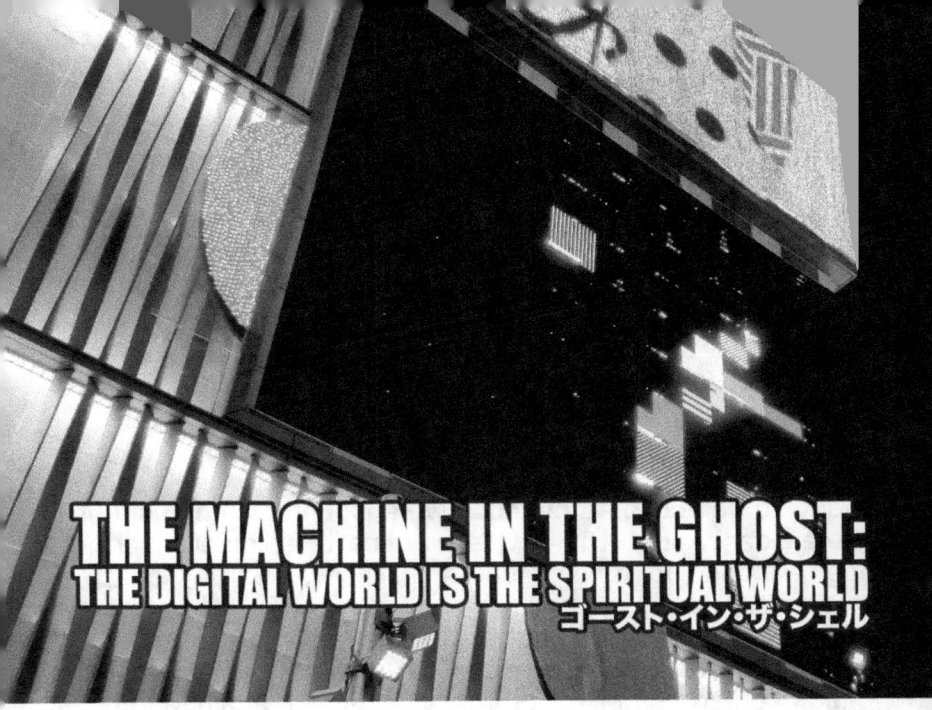

# THE MACHINE IN THE GHOST:
## THE DIGITAL WORLD IS THE SPIRITUAL WORLD
ゴースト・イン・ザ・シェル

By Ramirez De Leon

"Ghost in the Machine": A mechanical object, operated or inspired to motion by consciousness. Objects that move by an invisible, ghostlike force.

Human beings have a natural fascination, a need to involve themselves with spiritual practice. Human beings have been spiritual since the understanding that the sun, a mysterious, red ball of fire, granted life and light to the living.

This spiritual inclination or desire to build a relationship with the natural world beyond institutional science as we know it may be a natural phenomenon. That is, that human beings are naturally spiritual, they are naturally interested in the "beyond". And even at its most basic level, religion and spirituality can reinforce mankind's basic need for community.

In many developed nations, media and technology is the main way we communicate, experience, and learn. It is because of this, that even the atheist may now be exercising their hunger for spirituality through the interconnectedness of the internet. In a way, we project our spirit onto the digital, leaving our bodies to operate merely as mechanical objects. Our bodies have become machines, but our spirits are now projections into the digital ether.

It seems, the natural sciences, such as human biology, have taken a back seat to an oversimplified mechanical view of the body and its relationship to tech devices. Devices may be what we use to communicate with others but they are now apart of an internet-of-things. A whole of objects communicating with one another, wifi is now embedded into our architecture, and into our city-scape.

Today, to be accepted by those we encounter is not just our human desire, but it is now a practice of spiritual ritual or energetic feeding. It has become, for many, the true Godlike, magnetic pull.
Every day a new meme or video becomes a sort of temporary idol before quickly crumbling into obscurity. Digital content is only to be replaced by, yet again, another digital idol.

When we release our content into the digital, it is our ghost. It is our spirit that is supposed to represent what once was considered the emotion of the physical being. Today, the body is the machine that powers or operates this ghost, sending it out into different corners of consciousness, fading, searching, feeding...

"Where there was once the 'real,' there is now only the electronic generation and circulation of almost supernatural simulations. Where there was once stable human consciousness, there are now only the ghosts of fragmented, decentered, and increasingly schizophrenic subjectivities...."

— Prof. Jefferey Sconce [Excerpt From Grafton Tanner. "Babbling Corpse." (2016)]

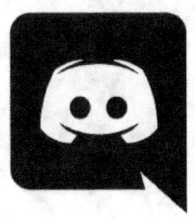 **DISCORD**

I had just cut my own hair. Q was making fun of it and then Nekkun came in strong with an album cover, and now I've used this little joke as an accuse to ask you to come hang out on the Discord.

Mostly at the moment it's pretty dead but we are moving some of the Visual Signals team to it to chat about articles, deadlines, etc. Also I'm constantly sharing daily news and new music that doesn't get into each issue.

We have a self-promotion channel were you can post your latest music in #music-share

Every so often, I do live interviews with future funk and vaporwave artists, which we always welcome people to listen in on. I'm not the best at building up a discord community, so I'm looking for some help. If Discord is your thing and you want to help grow the community, let's talk!

So of course, discord is a blast with friends - if you're not hanging out in the MTHU discord here's a code: z953nsA.

Anyways, I hope to see more people having fun. So come hang out!

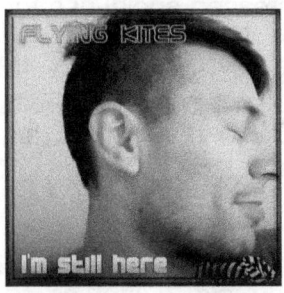 

**Flying Kites - I'm Still Here**

*early 1990s grunge with some experimental alt-rock* - Nekkun

*fresh, he got the panty droppin cut* - Q

*Damn... true* - me

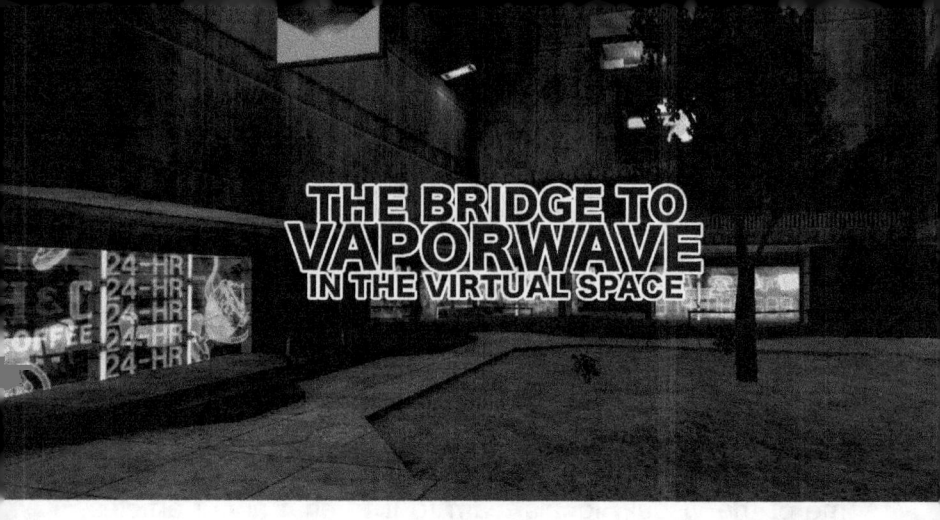

# THE BRIDGE TO VAPORWAVE
## IN THE VIRTUAL SPACE

By Ron De La Garza, Wave//Citizen

There are many culturally aesthetic tie-ins with vaporwave that attracts a listener's ears and eyes and seduces those who partake in it with feelings of nostalgia and a hazy reminiscence of themes not far from our past. These themes navigate our cultural memory through areas relating to found sound, accelerated commercialism, mid-era funk and jazz, and our earliest experiences with technology surrounding the surge and rise of the internet forming what we now call the digital age. The music that resides within this genre lies somewhere deep in a non-place, reminding us of things we remember vividly with a setting that we typically cannot pinpoint, a seemingly auditory backed liminal space.

Part of this aesthetic that has become richly ingrained in the genre's central themes, is the recalling of memories in our earliest virtual spaces. The concept of the virtual space lies within the beginning of the internet's increased social use for commentary, interaction, and enjoyment. The concept of the massively multiplayer game rose from these needs, and with them, many of the feelings of familiarity we get when we hear a Windows 98 boot sound or see GeoCities centric art inserted into any of these albums.

These early virtual places from the beginning of online interaction shine an aesthetic beacon on their own with their jagged polygons and midi laced soundtracks. Listening to pre-genre albums such as Far Side Virtual by James Ferraro

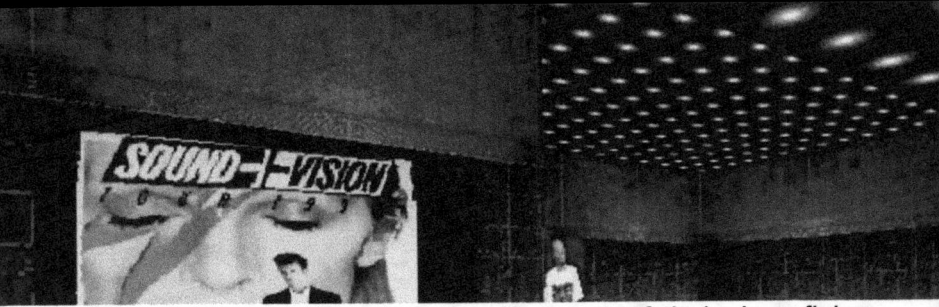

can induce nostalgic memories for many of their days flying through different worlds in Second Life. As a music almost rooted in nostalgia as its sonic motivator, vaporwave targets many corners in our memories. Many share collaborative experiences with these nostalgic triggers. We remember sitting in front of screens, watching the scan-lines run through our most worn video cassettes. Many remember downloading their media through peer2peer clients like Kazaa and LimeWire and blasting them through their Winamp player equipped with the best skin they could find. They sat at their desk grinding for levels in EverQuest, or even experienced strange encounters with anyone who also played Worlds.com. The midi heavy lush synths that we find in atmospheric works in vaporwave can weave synonymously with venturing the plains of the virtual worlds of our youth whether it be the cities of the Matrix online or the platformed forests of Maplestory.

The music that we find in this community is almost made, in a few occurrences, to highlight the experience of the modern computer user at the turn of the digital age. This is possibly due to many of the artists being from this era and time, or at least growing up with a piece of it in their memory. While the servers we used to populate are now empty and no longer filled with the vibrance of human avatars, the experiences shared within them still resonate. The musician takes what they know and shows this through their music. This can be seen in their curation of samples, choices in titles and the creation of their albums art. The niche of nostalgic centering we find in vaporwave's nod to video games, and 90s media is that anchor that many become attached to when they find this music for the first time. The memories that it keeps burning within us keeps us attached to the things we choose not to forget, and because of this, we will always still be grinding in the virtual worlds of the past, at least in spirit.

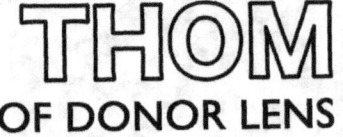 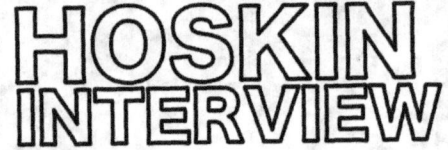

# THOM HOSKIN
## OF DONOR LENS
# INTERVIEW

By Aldo Lazcano // @GrooveRemote

Thom is a multi-instrumentalist and one half of Donor Lens. He also makes music under the moniker Love in Dust as well as Wichita Limewire. Additionally, with the help of his wife, he created the Groove Remote Radio musical theme heard at the beginning of the show.

**Could we start the interview by telling us some lesser known facts about you?**

I've always worked in music, apart from a brief period working as a tutor to the children of Russian oligarchs outside Moscow. I started out playing drums for British folk musicians including Laura Marling, and then had a stint in an indie band, but I've always felt electronic music was my natural home.

**How far does your background in music go and what was the first instrument you picked up?**

My mum is a piano teacher and used to play violin in local orchestras. I took up clarinet aged 7 at her suggestion, but asked for drum lessons as well when I was around 10. I got into synths and drum machines in my early teens when a family friend gave me his Roland SH-101; apparently his partner thought it was annoying and they reckoned I'd get more use out of it. I graduated onto 'proper' DAWs (Ableton Live version 4) around the same time, after a pre-history playing around with MTV Music Generator, eJay, and rhythm games like Dance Dance Revolution, Donkey Konga and PaRappa the Rapper. Guitar and other woodwinds I picked up much later, and I can't really remember a time when I didn't play piano, but I never formally studied it and my technique leaves a lot to be desired.

**How influential was your dad in your venture to becoming a musician?**

My dad was the only person at home who didn't play an instrument, and has only really got into music more recently. I'm very grateful for how tolerant he was of all the various noises in the house - my brother practiced tenor saxophone in one room while I was toying around with grooveboxes and a theremin in the attic. We even intercepted a neighbour taking an electric organ to the tip once, and added that to the collection of noise-makers.

The jobs he's worked have probably subconsciously led me to vaporwave. He had something to do with launching MTV in the UK, a long career in the video games industry and then moved to an audio-visual company. I had a stereotypically 90s childhood and was lucky enough to have some of the classic games and consoles at home (I have vivid memories of Sonic Adventure and Jet Set Radio on the Dreamcast, and 1080° Snowboarding on the N64). I think he's amused/bemused that Macintosh Plus sampled music from one of his titles (Turok) on the Floral Shoppe album.

**It seems that you and Jay are constantly collaborating, PowerPCME, DATAGIRL and Jana Tyrrell are some immediate recalls. Do you have a favorite collaboration? A dream collaboration?**

The Jana collab predates Donor Lens by many years. We were trying to make hyperpop under the name WorldAfloat around the time (2013/2014?) that PC Music was blowing up in the UK, and we'd both developed a simultaneous obsession with Kyary Pamyu Pamyu and Yasutaka Nakata's songwriting/production. That music never got properly released, but may still see the light of the day. We're very happy that the vaporwave community seems to enjoy the injection of pop Jana's voice brings, and I'm glad Jerome enjoys working with her as much as I do. She's an insanely talented producer in her own right and people will freak when they hear this Internet Club-meets-Charli XCX solo work she has brewing.

A dream collab would be to have Skylar Spence feature as a vocalist/co-writer on a track. We have a shared interest in Prefab

Sprout and 80s indie/sophisti-pop stuff, and it'd be so fun to make something together in that style.

**Being in the realm of vaporwave, do you see a more sophisticated marrying of Non-sampled vaporwave with jazz or any other genre of music?**

Honestly, the idea of 'sophistication' is something that I'm slightly wary of. I do like a lot of music that label gets applied to - Steely Dan, Japan, jazz, even some prog - but I don't think it makes it better than pop or dance music (and a lot of it is inadvertently quite funny or pretentious anyway). Within vaporwave, it's not inherently more skilful to make an original composition than to do something with samples, so long as it is imaginative and transformative. We get slightly bashful when people compliment our instrumental skills too, because it's not terribly relevant to making good vaporwave (and our friends who are virtuoso jazz, classical and metal musicians probably think we are terrible hacks by their standards!). We take our instrumental, production and writing practice seriously only because it allows us to write the music we want to. In the long run, if copyright rules are enforced more stringently, we are slightly future-proofed by being able to emulate the kind of sounds and grooves producers like to sample.

**Do you have any musical guilty pleasures?**

No, because I don't believe guilty pleasures are a thing! My Wichita LimeWire project is a love letter to music considered naff that nonetheless shaped me, for example. I really love Bassline House music from the UK, J-Pop like Kyary Pamyu Pamyu, and the frothiest disco imaginable. I don't trust people who pretend not to like 'Fairground' by Simply Red either.

**Besides Japanese whisky, what are some Donor Lens must-haves when working on new music?**

We normally work remotely because we live in different cities (London and Cardiff), so we need an internet connection and WeTransfer. When we do get to meet up in person to write, we drink cheap beers and eat spicy falafel wraps, but Jay got food poisoning one time so we've switched to what he calls 'vanilla dinners' or 'beige buffets'.

**How would you describe the Donor Lens sound? Is there any one thing that's integral to it?**

The most important thing is that there are two of us with pretty different personalities and tastes. I'm not saying we're on their level, but I really like the dynamics of duos like Outkast, Steely Dan, Knower, even British comedians like Vic Reeves & Bob Mortimer, where the two parts each bring something special and unique to the table.

The Donor Lens sound is a synthwave/metal producer (Jay), combining with someone who leans more towards ambient/experimental and pop music. Maybe vaporwave is the only genre where this collaboration makes any sense at all.

**When not working on Donor Lens or music in general, what are some other hobbies you have?**

Before the world ground to a halt, it was travel. In the last few years I've been to some pretty far-flung places in Asia, America and Europe. My wife would dispute that these trips are unrelated to music, though, as I'm always making field recordings. Both Donor Lens albums feature recordings of airports and convenience stores in Thailand, Taiwan and Hong Kong; and there's a Love in Dust track called 'Denki' that uses ambience captured from a modular synth-themed soba noodle restaurant in Osaka called Denki Soba.

**Lastly, What are you currently listening to?**

I'm completely enamoured with all the music emerging from this Louis Cole/Knower nexus of LA-based musicians: Genevieve Artadi, Sam Gendel, Sam Wilkes, Jacob Mann. The latest Kate NV album is amazing too. And Bill Frisell is a total master who has made one of his greatest records this year with Valentine. In the vapor world, Traipse has been a big discovery and I've heard previews of the new/final Power PCME album, which is staggeringly good.

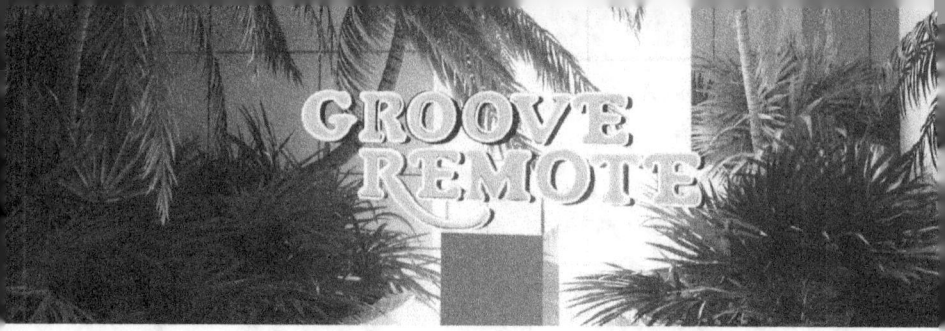

In collaboration with Visual Signals and GROOVE REMOTE, Thom Hoskin has put together a 30 minute guest mix to accompany the interview. Grab your phone, scan the QR code and listen to some of the best Love In Dust // Thom Hoskin jams.

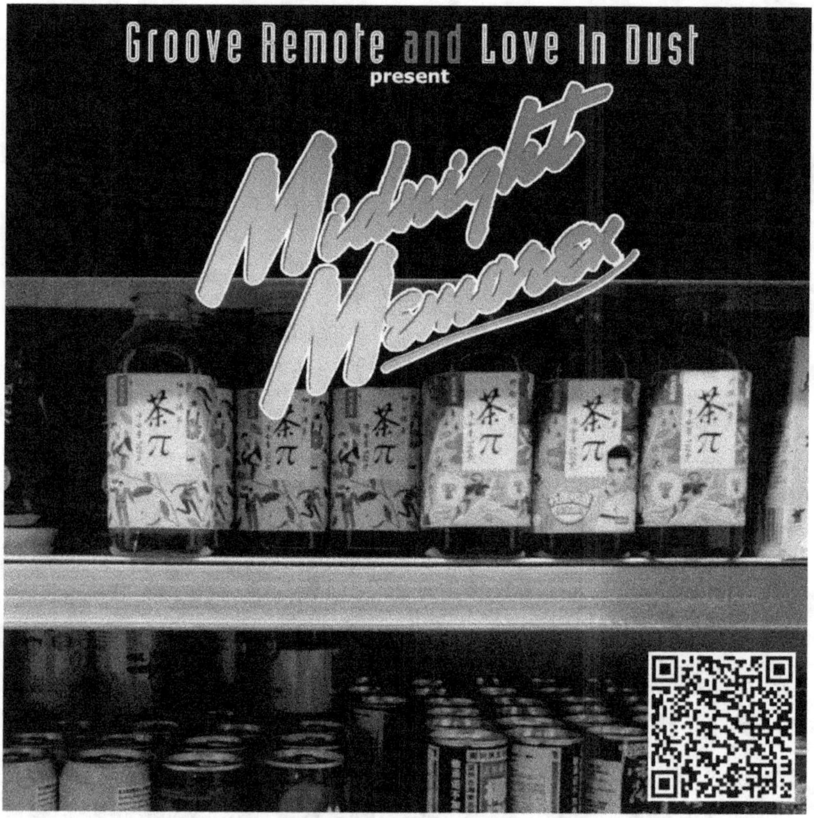

## Groove Remote and Love In Dust
### present
### Midnight Memorex

茶π 茶π 茶π 茶π 茶π 茶π

*Lastly, I want to thank Aldo Lazcano of @GrooveRemote for putting in so much time and effort to get this interview. They worked tirelessly over the weekend before publication organizing the interview and presenting in a readable form for this issue. Go give him a follow and check out the other Groove Remote mixes. — KITE0080*

# VISUAL ビジュアル SIGNALS
## merch

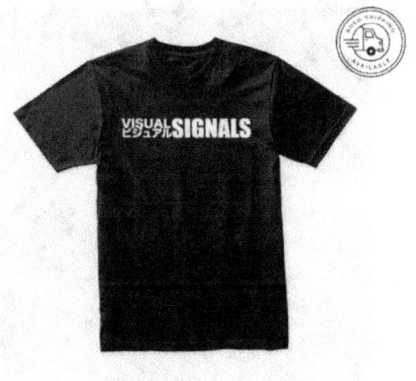

### Visual Signals T-Shirt
from **Musics The Hang Up**

**Product:** Premium Tee - $15.99 USD

**Description:**
Regular fit, unisex

~~View More Details~~

Select Size:     Quantity:

S               1

Colors:

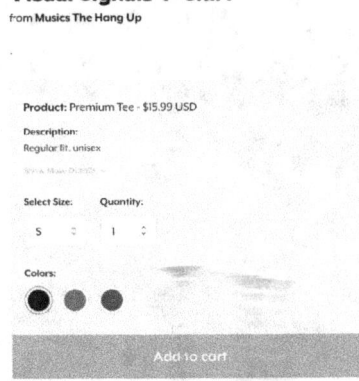

Add to cart

### visual signals hoodie
from **Musics The Hang Up**

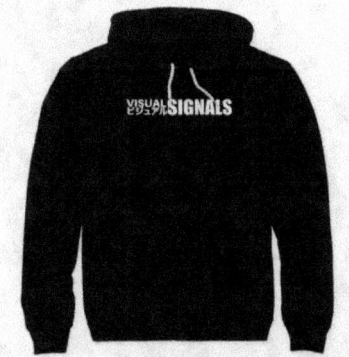

**Product:** Premium Pullover Hoodie - $29.99 USD

**Description:**
Regular fit, white drawcords, kangaroo pocket, unisex

~~View More Details~~

Select Size:     Quantity:

S               1

Colors:

Add to cart

Only on **Teespring**
http://visualsignals.xyz/merch

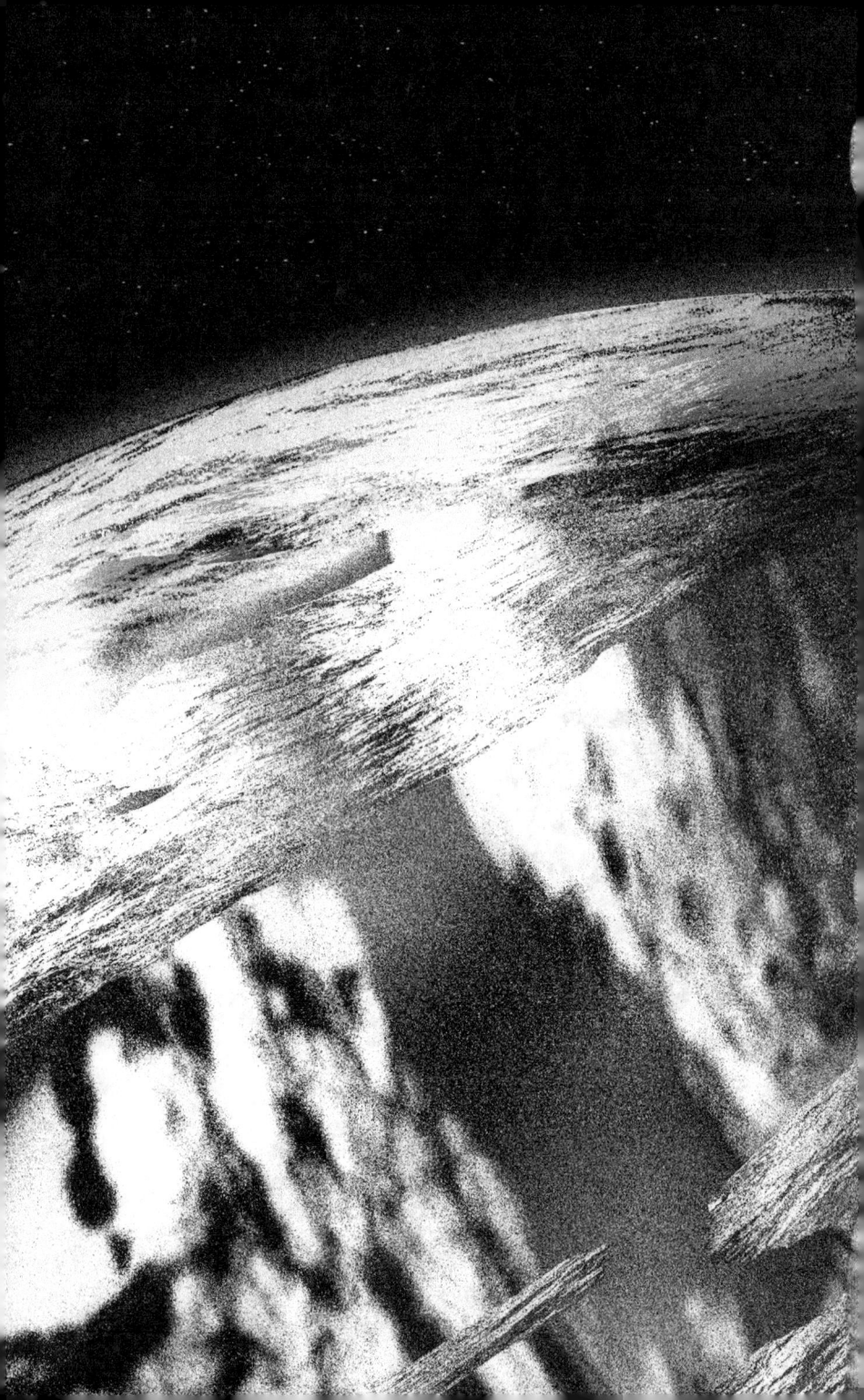

MAJESTY

# Issue Credits

All article / concepts / diagrams / ads / etc were developed by KITE0080 unless otherwise stated. But this project couldn't have existed without the following people:

**Credits:**
- All logos / brands / album art belong to their respective owners
- "DSi & 3DS Hacks Guide" by NightScript
  - https://nightyoshi370.github.io/
- "Big Music Promoters with their Small Ways To Promote" by Zico // @ZicoUWU
- "The Machine in the Ghost: The Digital World is the Spiritual World" - By Ramirez De Leon // @VRAM_CPU
- One day out of life... by KITE0080, image from Thought Adjuster's *You're Not Alone*
- Thom Hoskin Interview by Aldo Lazcano // @GrooveRemote
- "The Bridge To Vaporwave In the Virtual Space" by Wave//Citizen @WaveCitizenWave
- Majesty by an anonymous artist
- "5 horror themed Vaporwave albums for halloween" by By Jay Wallace // @jaywallace1
- Fan Collection by Petridisch

**Contact KITE0080 // MTHU**
- Twitter: @musicsthehangup // @SignalsVisual
- Instagram: @musicsthehangup
- Website: http://musicsthehangup.com
- Email: contact@musicsthehangup.com

**Join the official MTHU Discord:**
- http://musicsthehangup.com/discord

Do you have an amazing cassette collection? Let us know @SignalsVisual on Twitter and we might feature your collections in the next issue!

Do you ever get nervous some day some obscure vapor album you love will disappear? I get that feeling some times and that's why I always am trying to document that these albums existed... sorry if I don't write about the most popular tracks or artists. They will live on forever but some one off signalwave album might only last a few minutes and never get heard. If you know of an album like that let me know. I want to hear it and share it with our scene.

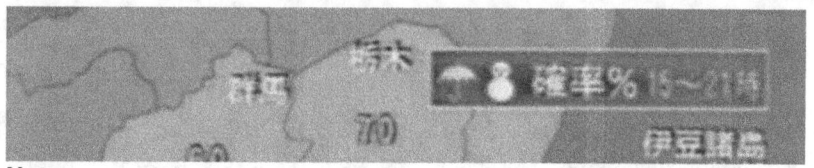

**Note:**
Every artist, label, project, album, opinion, thought, tweet, post, blog, YouTube video, anything anyone posts is not my opinion. Every one of these things belong to the respective artist / label. I don't know what horrific thing someone might say in the future either. Don't hold me liable for it.

Hey again my Future Friends,

Thanks again for supporting MTHU and Visual Signals. We actually now have 3 issues out in total! 2 more than I ever thought and I am loving every moment of it. This time around I met some really interesting people to help write some article. We have some better design and the overall feel of Visual Signals is becoming more refined. I hope you enjoyed the changes.

If you'd like to give some feedback, checkout this survey and let me know what you thought: https://www.surveymonkey.com/r/BZ82292

As always, if someone wrote something here that inspired you, go give them a follow and let them know. Everyone in each issue put in so much work and I know it'll make their day to know you enjoyed something they wrote. Thanks for everything everyone~

Cheers,
KITE0080 of MTHU

Cover Art Photography by KITE0080. An abandoned building near my old apartment at 八卦嶺.

Get your next copy automatically on Patreon:
https://www.patreon.com/visualsignals

## All Patreon Supporters
- Nekkun
- Sheep
- Jason VanSlycke
- eye click
- Rich Siegel
- Darkfez
- Dark5lalom
- Chiefahleaf
- Com_Zepol
- Vayu
- Yoshcko
- Joris Zynga

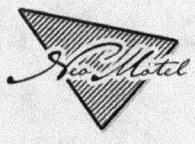

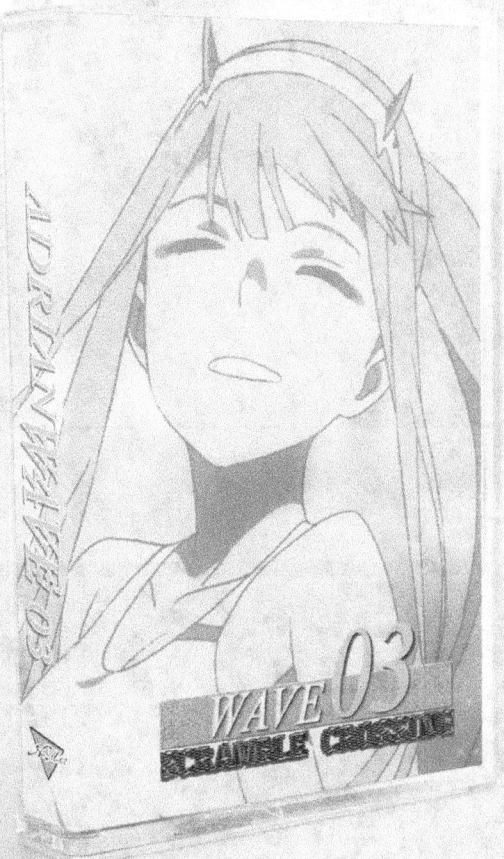

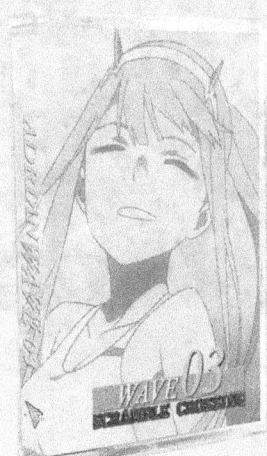

ADRIANWA
"WAVE03"
Limited Edition Cassette

August 7th 9PM (PDT)
August 8th 1PM (JST)

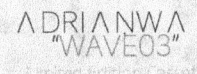

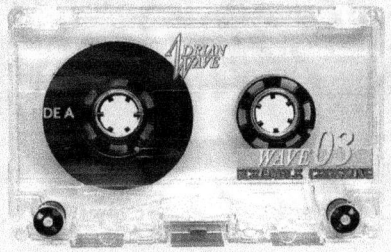

https://neomotel.bandcamp.com

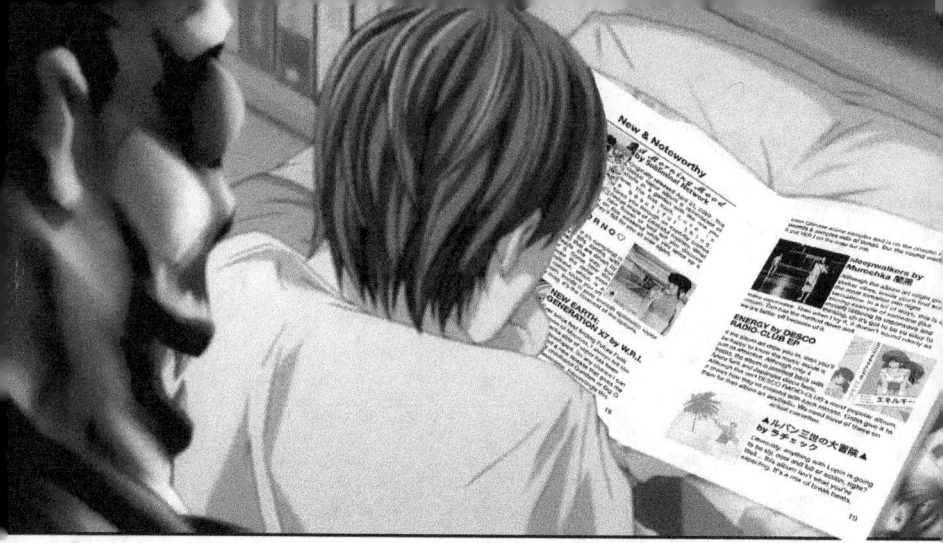

www.ingramcontent.com/pod-product-compliance
Lightning Source LLC
Chambersburg PA
CBHW071048220526
45467CB00004B/1732

*9 7 9 8 6 8 8 9 1 9 3 2 5 *

VISUAL
ビジュアル**SIGNALS**
ISSUE ONE

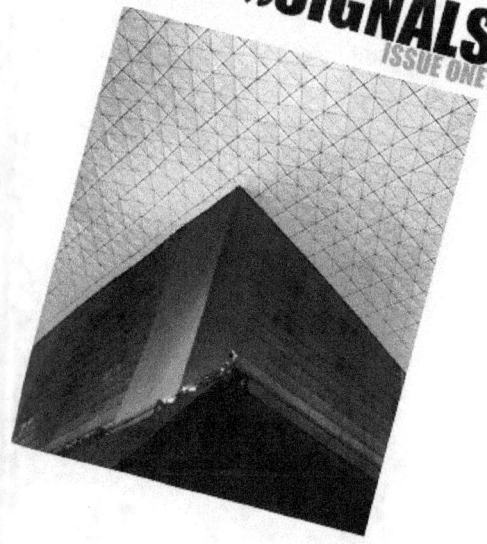

VISUAL
ビジュアル**SIGNALS**
ISSUE ZERO

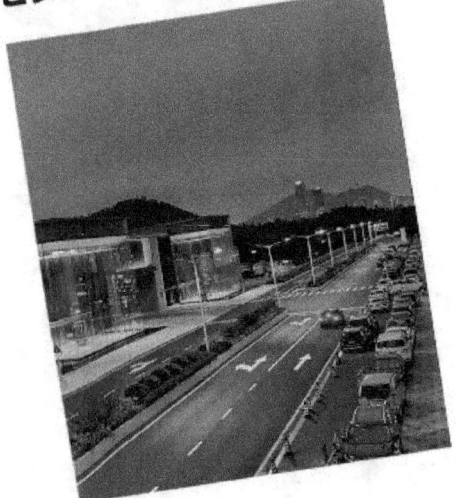